Walking in Truth™

A Biblical Worldview and Bible Survey Curriculum for Grades 6–8

The Christian Worldview

Student Workbook
Grade 6

Summit Ministries

Acknowledgements

Vice President of Program Services: Jason Graham

Managing Curriculum Editor: Macki Jones

Authors
John Hay, Jr.
Kim Pettit
Lorraine Wadman
Macki Jones

Editorial Team
John Conaway
Kim Pettit
Lorraine Wadman
Macki Jones
Nancy Sutton

Illustrator
Aline Heiser

Design Team
Claire Coleman
Mike Riester

Worldview Model Design
Randy Bounds
Steven Myasoto

Unless otherwise indicated, all Scripture quotations are taken from the *Holy Bible*, New Living Translation® (NLT®), copyright© 2018 by Tyndale House Foundation. Used by permission of Tyndale House Publishers, Inc., Carol Stream, Illinois 60188. All rights reserved.

International Children's Bible®, copyright© 1986, 1988, 1999, 2015 by Tommy Nelson™, a division of Thomas Nelson, Inc. Used by permission. All rights reserved.

Published by Summit Press, P.O. Box 207, Manitou Springs, CO 80829
Fourth Printing (2023)
Printed in India

ISBN-13: 978-1-7330256-0-7

Walking in Truth Table of Contents—Student Workbook

Getting Started

1. Write the words to Colossians 2:8. _____
_____
_____

2. Jorge, Sandy, Antoinette, and Theo are looking at the picture to the left. Jorge, Sandy, and Antoinette all see the tree. Theo sees two profiles of people. Does this mean that Theo is wrong? _____

3. Is Theo seeing the picture correctly? _____

4. Are Jorge, Sandy, and Antoinette seeing the picture correctly? _____

5. Explain why Jorge and his friends are all seeing the picture correctly. _____
_____
_____

Nelson and Latasha are looking at a field of beautiful wildflowers. Nelson is wearing green glasses. Latasha is wearing clear glasses. Both of them are looking at the same field.

6. Does Nelson see the flowers as they really are? _____

7. Does Latasha see the flowers as they really are? _____

8. Explain how Nelson sees the field of flowers and why. _____
_____
_____

9. Explain how Latasha sees the field of flowers and why. _____
_____
_____

10. Explain what Nelson has to do in order to see the field of flowers as it really is. _____
_____
_____

11. Zach, Emelia, and Enrique are all trying to make sense of life and the world. What do the glasses they are wearing represent? _____

_____

_____

12. What five categories of questions do Zach, Emelia, and Enrique need to answer as they seek to make sense of their world?

a. _____   b. _____

c. _____   d. _____

e. _____

13. Think of one question from each of the five question categories that you would like to ask.

Question Categories	My Questions
_____	_____
_____	_____
_____	_____
_____	_____
_____	_____

14. Choose one of your questions from above. Place a star by the question. Choose someone in your school whom you think would answer the question accurately. Explain why you chose that person to answer your question. Finally, explain how that person might answer your question.

_____

_____

_____

_____

_____

_____

_____

1. What is a worldview? _____

_____

_____

_____

A.

B.

2. What do you think the person helping the other person in Picture A believes about people?

_____

_____

_____

3. How would you expect the person in Picture A to act toward others?

_____

_____

_____

4. What do you think the group of four teens in Picture B believes about people?

_____

_____

5. How would you expect the people in Picture B to act toward others?

_____

_____

_____

All worldviews include five groups or categories of beliefs. First, write the category of worldview belief each picture represents. Next, identify two different, or opposing, beliefs that people hold for each category. Finally, write a belief you hold for each category.

6. All worldviews include beliefs about _____

One belief _____

An opposing belief _____

A belief I hold _____

7. All worldviews include beliefs about _____

One belief _____

An opposing belief _____

A belief I hold _____

8. All worldviews include beliefs about _____

One belief _____

An opposing belief _____

A belief I hold _____

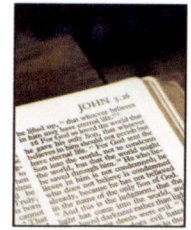

9. All worldviews include beliefs about _____

One belief _____

An opposing belief _____

A belief I hold _____

10. All worldviews include beliefs about _____

One belief _____

An opposing belief _____

A belief I hold _____

I Believe...

1. List the four ways in which we acquire our beliefs.

a. _____

b. _____

c. _____

d. _____

2. Read the scenarios below. Identify which of the four ways the individual acquired his or her belief.

a. Derek's parents always encourage him to tell the truth. Derek believes that telling the truth is the right thing to do. He also believes that lying is wrong. Derek acquired this belief through

_____.

b. Sonya reads her Bible every day. She believes that God's Word is the Truth. She also believes that God is the Creator of the universe and everything in it. Sonya acquired this belief through

_____.

c. Jamil was eating lunch with a group of people he didn't know very well. As he listened to the conversations, he discovered that not all people believe in heaven and hell, and he began to think that they might be right. Jamil acquired this belief through

_____.

d. Maya's best friend loves to make up fictional stories. One day, she told Maya that there are hundreds of gods that rule the universe. Each god has a job. If you want it to rain, you have to pray to the rain god. If someone was sick, he or she would have to request healing from the medicine god. Maya thought about this for a long time and decided that her friend was right. Maya believes that there are many gods that we need to pray to. Maya acquired this belief through

_____.

There are four ways in which people acquire their worldview. Write about two beliefs you have come to hold through each of these four ways.

3. Beliefs I have acquired by observation: _____

_____

_____

_____

4. Beliefs I have acquired through teaching: _____

_____

_____

_____

5. Beliefs I have acquired through personal study: _____

_____

_____

_____

6. Beliefs I have acquired through reasoning and imagination: _____

_____

_____

_____

1. What are the five "ingredients" that make up a person's worldview?

a. _____

b. _____

c. _____

d. _____

e. _____

2. Read the statements. Write **T** for true and **F** for false.

_____ a. Having a worldview helps a person make choices.

_____ b. People deliberately develop their worldview.

_____ c. A person's worldview helps him or her understand life and the world.

_____ d. A worldview influences how a person acts or behaves.

3. Your friend is having a difficult time trying to make sense of the world. She believes many things, but she's having trouble sorting, or categorizing, her beliefs. You decide to use the illustration of a cake to help her think more clearly about what she believes. What would you say to your friend?

_____

_____

_____

_____

_____

_____

_____

_____

_____

_____

4. Describe the changes you see in each picture.

_____   _____

_____   _____

5. Now think about some of the changes in your life. List three ways you have changed since you were born.

_____

_____

_____

6. Think about some of your beliefs about life and the world. Have any of them changed from when you were very young? List two beliefs that have changed. _____

_____

_____

7. What worldview beliefs about people do you think these students hold?

_____

_____

_____

_____

8. What worldview beliefs about people do you think the boys in the picture have? _____

_____

_____

_____

1. List three reasons why your worldview matters. Give an example of each reason.

Reason 1: _____

_____

Example: _____

_____

_____

Reason 2: _____

_____

Example: _____

_____

_____

Reason 3: _____

_____

Example: _____

_____

_____

2. List four powerful influences in your everyday life that can affect your worldview and take your thoughts captive.

a. _____

b. _____

c. _____

d. _____

3. Identify one of those four influences that you know has affected your worldview or what you believe. Give an example.

My worldview has been influenced by:

_____

Example: _____

_____

_____

_____

_____

_____

_____

_____

Much of what we see, read, and hear influences our worldview. Read the two scenarios below. Then explain some of the worldview beliefs the advertisement and the health book are communicating. Explain why you agree or disagree. Be careful—often truthful and untruthful messages are mixed together in what we see, read, and hear.

4. The first scene of a television commercial shows an unhappy person driving an older, brown model car. The second scene shows the same person smiling while sitting in a brand-new silver sports car. Many people are gathered around him, admiring the car and asking for a ride. The commercial ends with this slogan: "Bored with your ordinary life? Buy a Sportaratti and start living an exciting life today!"

Worldview beliefs communicated in this commercial: _____

_____

_____

_____

Why I agree or disagree: _____

_____

_____

5. You read in your health book that it's important to develop a healthy mind and self-image. To do this, the book says you must decide what you want to become. Then you must put your mind to it and think positively. You have the strength within yourself to do and become anything you wish. Most importantly, you must never let other people tell you what is best for you.

Worldview beliefs communicated in the health book: _____

_____

_____

_____

Why I agree or disagree: _____

_____

_____

1. Write the words to Romans 1:20, the memory verse. _____

_____

_____

2. Distinguish between theism and monotheism. _____

_____

3. Name the three major world religions that are based on the belief of monotheism.

a. _____

b. _____

c. _____

4. Explain the difference between the Jewish, Christian, and Islamic beliefs about God.

a. Judaism: _____

_____

_____

b. Christianity: _____

_____

_____

c. Islam: _____

_____

_____

5. Fill in the blanks. Use your Student Textbook for help.

Three of the main monotheistic religions of the world share a common belief that there is only one God.

All three worldviews believe that God is the Creator of the _____.

Jews and Muslims believe that God is a personal Creator. Christians believe that God is three in

_____, the Father, Son, and Holy Spirit, yet one God. All three

worldviews acknowledge that God is all-powerful, all-knowing, _____,

and absolutely _____.

6. Jews, Christians, and Muslims all believe their monotheistic worldview is based on revelation from God. However, each religion has a different understanding of God's revelation. Explain each religion's beliefs about how God has revealed himself. Explain how these views are alike and how they are different.

a. Judaism: _____

_____

_____

_____

_____

b. Christianity: _____

_____

_____

_____

_____

c. Islam: _____

_____

_____

_____

_____

_____

7. Match the book or books that each of these three monotheistic worldview religions identifies as God's special revelation.

The Old and New Testaments of the Bible _____

The Torah and other Hebrew Scriptures _____

The Quran as well as parts of the Old
and New Testaments, including the Psalms _____

A. Islam

B. Christianity

C. Judaism

Match the statements to the worldview that each speaker holds.

1. _____ "I don't believe in anything outside
of what can be scientifically proven to exist."

2. _____ "I believe that I am god, you are god, and that
every rock, tree, and animal are god."

3. _____ "I believe that when all people open their minds
to the god force and meditate, the world will
finally be in harmony."

4. _____ "Science proves that there is no God."

| A. New spirituality |
| B. Naturalism |

5. Read Romans 1:20. What does this verse say to people who hold an atheistic or naturalistic worldview?

_____

_____

_____

Read each statement below and check the worldview associated with it.

	New Spirituality	Naturalism
6. Unless it can be proven by science, it doesn't exist.		
7. All is god and god is all.		
8. Our five senses deny God's existence.		
9. There is no God.		
10. God is an energy or a force for good.		

11. Your friend believes that meditation, chanting, and wearing a crystal pendant will unify her spirit with the god force of the universe. How would you categorize her worldview? Read 1 Corinthians 8:6 and John 14:6 and tell how these verses relates to your friend's worldview.

_____

_____

_____

_____

12. In the first section, explain how Christianity's view of God differs from the naturalistic view of God. In the second section, explain how Christianity's view of God differs from new spirituality's view of God.

The Biblical View of God Versus the Naturalistic View of God

_____

_____

_____

_____

_____

_____

_____

The Biblical View of God Versus the New Spirituality Movement's View of God

_____

_____

_____

_____

_____

_____

_____

13. Write on the lines below each image the worldview most closely associated with it.

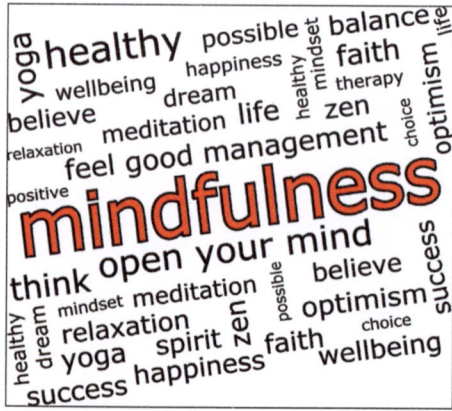

_____   _____   _____

Getting Started and Topic 1

1. Explain why telling stories is such a big part of our lives. _____

_____

_____

2. Read the story. Answer the questions.

Megan and Sierra were together through elementary school, but Sierra is not going to attend Megan's school anymore. Megan is upset. Sierra is her best friend. Sierra and her family are moving so her parents can work as missionaries overseas. Megan knows her mother does not think it is important to tell people about God. She thinks everyone should believe whatever they want. Megan agrees with her. Sierra was a great friend, and Megan will miss her. Megan thinks that if moving away from your friends were the right thing to do, it wouldn't hurt so much.

a. What does Megan believe about God? _____

_____

b. What does Megan believe about truth? _____

_____

c. What does Megan believe about right and wrong? _____

_____

_____

d. What different beliefs might make Megan happy about her friend's move? _____

_____

3. What are the themes of God's great story? Circle the letter of your choice.

   a. Father, Son, Spirit   b. God, cosmos, people, truth, values   c. creation, fall, redemption

4. Write the definition of creation. _____

_____

5. Renumber the pictures in the order they should go according to Genesis 1.

_____   _____   _____   _____   _____

_____   _____   _____   _____

6. Write the words to Colossians 1:19–20. _____

_____

_____

7. Study the picture. Write the truths that correspond to each symbol.

a. Upper hand above the earth: _____

_____

b. Animals, plants, people, planets: _____

_____

c. Angels, air, space: _____

_____

d. Lower hand under the earth: _____

_____

e. People wearing crowns and banner: _____

_____

f. Musical staff and notes: _____

_____

1. Study the picture. Write the truths about the creation that correspond to each symbol.

a. Musical staff and notes: _____

_____

b. Faces and hands turned toward God: _____

_____

c. Happy faces and white robes of purity: _____

_____

d. Man and woman holding hands: _____

_____

e. Fruitfulness of the earth; the lion and lamb together: _____

_____

f. Uneaten fruit in lower left corner: _____

_____

2. Study the pictures. Which truths from the answers to Exercise 1 does each picture represent?

a. _____

_____

_____

_____

_____

_____

_____

_____

_____

b. _____

_____

_____

_____

_____

_____

_____

_____

3. Colossians 1:17 and Hebrews 1:3 are verses that speak of God's sustaining power. What are some ways that you see God sustaining his creation? _____

_____

_____

4. Read Psalm 104:24–30. Answer the questions.

a. What did God create? _____

b. According to these verses, how does God sustain his creation? _____

_____

_____

c. What phrase in this passage shows that people need fellowship with God? _____

_____

d. Which verse in this passage relates to Genesis 2:7? _____

5. Cross out the extra words in the definition of the creation.

The stars and planets in the heavens and the earth and everything tangible in them, both only visible and not invisible, created out of primordial matter nothing divine essence by the word power will chance of the unknown big bang God and independent from sustained by him.

6. Who is the person mentioned in your memory verse, Colossians 1:19–20? _____

7. What does he accomplish? _____

_____

8. God created four relationships to be in harmony. Describe what each relationship means to you.

a. Harmony with God _____

_____

b. Harmony with self _____

_____

c. Harmony with others _____

_____

d. Harmony with the earth _____

_____

1. Fill in the missing words in the definition of the fall.

The _____ of _____ into the

_____ and the disobedience of _____ and _____ .

2. In your own words, describe what happened in the fall. _____

_____

_____

3. Study the picture. Write the truths about the fall that correspond to each symbol.

a. The eaten fruit: _____

_____

b. The broken notes: _____

_____

c. People facing away from the light of God: _____

_____

_____

d. People's faces and postures reflecting despair: _____

_____

e. Glaring faces, clenched fists: _____

_____

f. Pollution; dry, cracked soil; thorns: _____

_____

4. When sin entered creation, it produced disharmony in the four relationships of creation. Describe how disharmony in each relationship continues today.

a. Between people and God: _____

_____

_____

b. Within each person: _____

_____

_____

c. Among people: _____

_____

_____

d. With the earth: _____

_____

_____

5. Read the story. Complete the questions.

Mateo is annoyed. His mother signed him and his sister up to help clean up the park. He is tired of picking up trash. He thinks most people are sloppy and that he should not have to waste his Saturday cleaning up other people's messes. He would rather be having fun and playing with his friends.

a. What attitude does Mateo have toward other people? _____

_____

b. Is Mateo right? Why or why not? _____

_____

c. What evidence does Mateo have to show disharmony among people and the earth? _____

_____

d. How might you encourage Mateo? _____

_____

6. In each row, circle the verse that discusses sin in that relationship of creation.

a. Between people and God	Exodus 15:2	Micah 7:9	1 Chronicles 16:25
b. Within each person	Exodus 3:11	Psalm 38:3	Ecclesiastes 2:24
c. Among people	John 15:17	Hebrews 10:24	Psalm 25:19
d. With the earth	Psalm 8:9	Psalm 24:1	Revelation 11:18

1. Cross out the extra words in the definition of God's plan for redemption.

God's intent plan to ratify redeem and reverse the restoration direction of harmony in each development in relationship of history creation through the penalty payment of human beings' suffering Jesus' death daily on the cross and in the church his resurrection.

2. In your own words, describe God's plan for redemption. _____

_____

_____

_____

3. Study the picture. What symbols correspond to each truth?

a. The cross: _____

_____

_____

b. Uplifted hands and faces: _____

_____

_____

c. Joy in people's faces: _____

_____

_____

d. Groups of people in fellowship: _____

_____

e. Fruit and greenness of nature: _____

_____

_____

4. To reconcile is to restore to friendship or harmony. Circle the verses that discuss this concept.

Romans 5:10   Exodus 1:10   2 Corinthians 5:18   James 4:4   John 15:15

5. Are redemption and reconciliation the same thing? Explain._____

_____

_____

6. Read the Scriptures on the left. Write the name of the theme to which they refer—**creation**, **the fall**, or **redemption**. Then write the name of the relationship of creation to which they refer—with **God**, with **self**, with **others**, or with **the earth**.

	Theme	Relationship
a. Adam blamed God for giving him Eve, and he blamed Eve for giving him the fruit, which he ate. Genesis 3:12	_____	_____
b. God decided that it was not good at all for the man to be alone, so he made someone just right to help him. Genesis 2:18	_____	_____
c. Jesus Christ is the head of the church, and the church is his body. Colossians 1:18	_____	_____
d. God called out, asking where Adam was. Genesis 3:9	_____	_____
e. Anyone who belongs to Christ is made into a brand-new person. The old ways are gone; it is the start of a whole new life. 2 Corinthians 5:17	_____	_____
f. We wait for God's promised new heavens and new earth, which will be full of God's holiness. 2 Peter 3:13	_____	_____

7. Read Isaiah 65:17–25. Explain how it shows harmony in each of the four relationships.

_____

_____

_____

_____

Getting Started and Topics 1–3

1. Write the words of Isaiah 33:6. _____

_____

_____

_____

2. Answer the questions on the basis of Isaiah 33:6.

a. Who or what will bring us stability or a sure foundation for our life? _____

b. Besides a firm, stable foundation, what else will we receive?

_____

_____

_____

c. What blessing comes from a "fear" or respect for the Lord? _____

_____

3. Fill in the circle in front of the statement that is true about God's Word.

○ Jesus' words can be found in the Bible.

○ Biblical truths are good advice, but not essential for building a strong life.

○ Other teachings, such as the Quran, provide us with instruction that is equal to biblical wisdom.

○ God's Word is too difficult to understand and apply to our life.

Biblical Truth 2

Biblical Truth 3

Biblical Truth 4

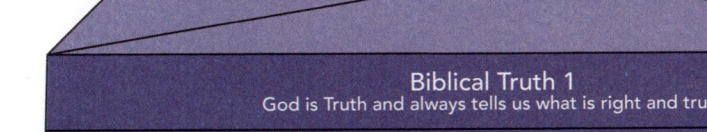

Biblical Truth 1
God is Truth and always tells us what is right and true.

THE FOUNDATION OF WISDOM
Knowing, loving, and obeying God, my Rock

THE ROCK
God and his Word

4. Write the four stones of Biblical Truths that make up the Foundation of Truth.

a. Biblical Truth 1: _____

b. Biblical Truth 2: _____

c. Biblical Truth 3: _____

d. Biblical Truth 4: _____

Match each Biblical Truth to its key verse.

5. Biblical Truth 1 _____

6. Biblical Truth 2 _____

7. Biblical Truth 3 _____

8. Biblical Truth 4 _____

A. Isaiah 45:19c

B. Ephesians 3:9c

C. Psalm 86:10

D. 2 Corinthians 13:14

Read the verses. Make an **X** in the column that shows the way God reveals himself to us.

	Through Creation	Through the Bible	Through Jesus Christ
9. All Scripture is breathed out by God. (2 Timothy 3:16)			
10. The heavens declare the glory of God, and the sky above proclaims his handiwork. (Psalm 19:1)			
11. In these last days he has spoken to us by his Son. (Hebrews 1:2)			

1. What does The Wall of Fellowship represent? _____

_____

BUILDING ON THE ROCK
"Everyone who hears my words and obeys them is like a man who built his house on rock." Matthew 7:24

Biblical Truth 5	Biblical Truth 6	Biblical Truth 7	Biblical Truth 8
God created people to be his children and to praise his glory	God created people to need him for everything	Sin causes separation and disharmony between people and God	Jesus died to restore fellowship and harmony between people and God

THE WALL OF FELLOWSHIP
A relationship of harmony with God when I believe that Jesus is God's Son and my Savior

Biblical Truth 1
God is Truth and always tells us what is right and true

THE FOUNDATION OF WISDOM
Knowing, loving, and obeying God, my Rock

THE ROCK
God and his Word

2. Match the Scriptures to each Biblical Truth. Read each verse and write its reference(s) on the line.

a. Biblical Truth 5 _____

b. Biblical Truth 6 _____

c. Biblical Truth 7 _____

d. Biblical Truth 8 _____

2 Timothy 1:9
1 John 1:8, Romans 3:23
Ephesians 1:5, 12
Acts 17:25

3. Read Talia and Jon's conversation. Write **Biblical Truth 5**, **Biblical Truth 6**, **Biblical Truth 7**, or **Biblical Truth 8**, whichever applies to the comment made.

Jon: I don't believe people were made for any reason. We just appeared. _____

Talia: Actually, we were made to praise God. _____

Jon: I doubt that. We don't need God. We can have a great life without him. _____

Talia: We need God for everything. Even our talents come from God. _____

Jon: That seems unlikely. I don't think anything God does or has done in the past, including Jesus' death on the cross, has any meaning for people today. _____

Talia: People today still sin and experience separation from God. _____

Fill in the circle in front of the best choice to complete each sentence.

4. Biblical Truth 6 affirms that God created people to need him for _____.

○ peace   ○ everything   ○ hope   ○ patience

5. Biblical Truth 7 says that sin caused destruction of the harmony between people and _____.

○ others   ○ God   ○ animals   ○ nature

6. Biblical Truth 8 says that Jesus' death on the cross restored _____.

○ harmony and fellowship   ○ peace   ○ opportunity   ○ grace

7. Read 1 John 1:3. Answer the questions.

a. With whom did God create us to have fellowship? _____

b. How is it possible to have fellowship with God and with Jesus even though we sin? _____

_____

_____

8. Complete the Wall of Fellowship crossword puzzle.

Across
3 made
5 bring back
6 pulled away; split
8 more than one child

Down
1 a relationship of harmony with God
2 God's amazing awesomeness
4 to tell God how wonderful he is
7 to be required

1. Write the words to the Biblical Truth pillars in the Wall of Image-Bearing.

a. Biblical Truth 9: _____

b. Biblical Truth 10: _____

c. Biblical Truth 11: _____

d. Biblical Truth 12: _____

2. Match the key Scriptures to each Biblical Truth. Read each verse and write its reference on the line.

a. Biblical Truth 9 _____

b. Biblical Truth 10 _____

c. Biblical Truth 11 _____

d. Biblical Truth 12 _____

| Isaiah 57:21 |
| Genesis 5:1b |
| 2 Corinthians 5:17 |
| Psalm 8:5 |

3. Underline all the ways we bear God's image.

We attend worship services.   We have minds to think.

We have the ability to make choices.   We have a conscience to discern right from wrong.

We have emotions.   We have rights and freedoms.

4. Read Psalm 8:5–8. Answer the questions.

a. With what are we crowned? _____ and _____

b. What responsibilities do God's image-bearers have respect to creation? _____

_____

c. What God-honoring abilities do God's image-bearers have that animals do not have? _____

_____

_____

d. To whom did God give the ability to live forever with him, human beings or animals?

_____

BUILDING ON THE ROCK
"Everyone who hears my words and obeys them is like a man who built his house on rock." Matthew 7:24

Biblical Truth 9	Biblical Truth 10	Biblical Truth 11	Biblical Truth 12
God created all people in his image	God placed a crown of glory and honor on his image-bearers	Sin causes disharmony within God's image-bearers	Jesus died to restore harmony within God's image-bearers

THE WALL OF IMAGE-BEARING
A relationship of harmony with myself as I become more like Jesus

Biblical Truth 2
God is the only true and almighty God

THE FOUNDATION OF WISDOM
Knowing, loving, and obeying God, my Rock

THE ROCK
God and his Word

5. Read the paraphrase of Psalm 32:3–5. King David wrote these words about his guilt over his sin with Bathsheba and his attempted cover-up for his sin. Underline the physical effects that David experienced as a result of guilt.

When I denied my sin, my bones started to dissolve,

   because I experienced the weight of guilt all day.

All day and night, you reminded me of my sin;

   my strength disappeared as if it were summertime.

But then I confessed my sin,

   And didn't try to hide it from you;

 I said, "The Lord needs to hear my confession,"

   and you heard and forgave my sin.

Read the statements. Decide whether they are true or false on the basis of Biblical Truths 9–12. Write the number of the Biblical Truth that confirms your opinion.

	True or False	Biblical Truth
6. A human being is a higher form of animal that has evolved randomly over billions of years.		
7. All people make mistakes, but their hearts are basically good.		
8. The life of an animal is equally important and valuable as the life of a human being.		
9. All people have worth and value because they are created in God's image.		
10. People have the strength within to have personal harmony without God.		
11. People cannot have true inner peace and harmony without a relationship with Christ.		
12. When people receive Jesus as their Savior, God replaces their guilt with forgiveness, and they are no longer subject to eternal separation from him.		

1. Read the memory verse, Isaiah 33:6. Answer the following questions.

a. How does knowing God's Word provide stability for your life? _____

_____

b. Jesus set an example of servanthood for us. Is serving others an important part of building a strong life? Why or why not? _____

_____

_____

Read the verses that apply to Biblical Truths 13 and 14 below. Match the verse to the correct truth by writing the number of the truth on the line.

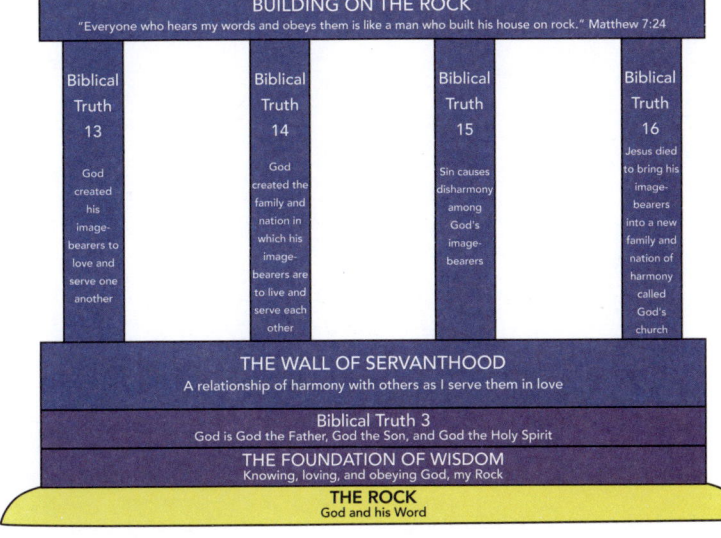

2. _____ Genesis 12:2

3. _____ Ecclesiastes 4:9–10

4. _____ Acts 17:26

5. _____ Matthew 23:11

6. _____ 1 John 3:16

7. _____ 1 Peter 2:9

8. Underline the requirements for godly service.

sacrifice	serving friends only	being considerate
meeting needs	following Christ's example	selfishness
serving enemies	concern for others' welfare	humility

God created the families and nations in which his image-bearers are to live and serve each other. Write **nation** or **family** on the line as it applies.

9. God sets the boundaries for its existence.

_____

10. God gave the first human beings the responsibility to create this.

_____

11. Write the words of Biblical Truth 15 and then answer the questions.

_____

_____

a. Describe some of the effects of disharmony among God's image-bearers that you have seen in your own community.

_____

_____

_____

b. What are examples of disharmony that are evident in our nation? _____

_____

_____

12. Write the words of Biblical Truth 16 and then answer the questions: _____

_____

a. How did disharmony come into the world? _____

b. How did Jesus defeat Satan and restore harmony to creation? _____

_____

_____

c. What is Christ's holy nation? _____

d. What is God's church made up of? _____

e. Describe some of the things that members of your church do to serve others. _____

_____

_____

f. As a new creation in Christ, list several ways that you can serve your family.

_____   _____

_____   _____

_____   _____

g. List ways you can serve your church or school.

_____   _____

_____   _____

_____   _____

_____   _____

Use the Word Bank to complete the sentences about stewardship.

1. _____ is building a relationship of harmony with the earth as I appreciate it and rule over it.

2. God _____ the earth and all that is in it.

3. People have a _____ to care for the earth.

4. Plants and animals _____ after their own kind.

5. Coal, oil, land, and forests are _____.

6. Although we are stewards over God's creation, the _____ of the earth is still God's.

7. When Christ returns, he will _____ the earth.

Word Bank
renew
sustains
reproduce
stewardship
natural resources
ownership
responsibility

8. Biblical Truth 17 affirms that God holds creation together by his power. Underline the things God sustains.

   the rotation of the earth   traffic patterns

   boundaries for the seas   Earth's orbit

   the moon and planetary movements   gravity

   our breath   justice and governance

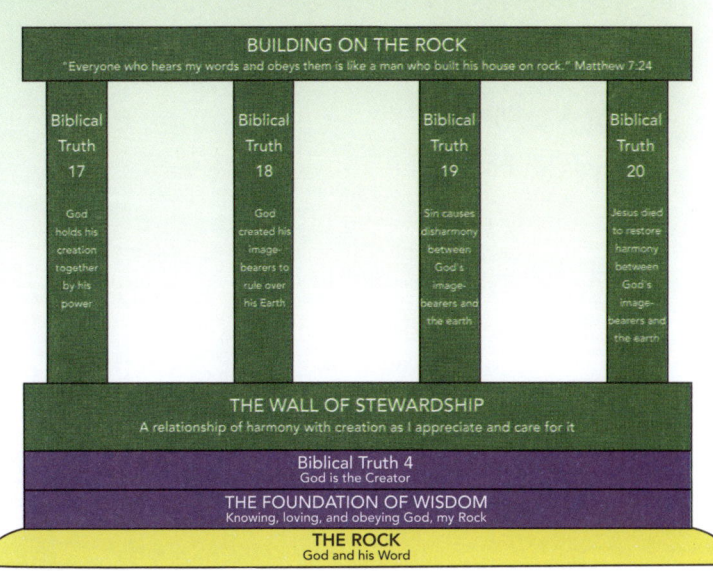

Determine whether the statements below are a part of God's mandate to his image-bearers to rule over the earth or not. Write **true** or **false** on the lines.

9. _____ God's image-bearers are to care for the earth's plant and animal life.

10. _____ People and animals are equally capable of stewardship responsibilities.

11. _____ Good stewardship often requires thoughtful design for the wise use of resources and deliberate planning for the future.

12. _____ Stewardship only applies to the earth as a whole and not to our own environments at home, school, and in our local community.

13. Complete the chart by writing the phrases found below in the appropriate columns.

Biblical Truth 17	Biblical Truth 18	Biblical Truth 19	Biblical Truth 20

new heavens and new earth

weeds and natural disasters

the orderly rotation and orbit of the earth

new bodies that will never decay

Christ's defeat of death and Satan

selfish misuse and abuse of natural resources

animal reproduction after their own kind

the mandate to fill the earth with people

people with authority over animal life

air pollution, water pollution, and litter

14. What are ways that sixth graders can use natural resources wisely? List a minimum of six ways.

_____   _____

_____   _____

_____   _____

15. Read Revelation 21:1–8. List eight types of persons or things that will not be in the New Jerusalem.

_____

_____

_____

_____

_____

_____

_____

_____

Read the character traits for obedience, joy, trust, humility, and compassion. Then read the following verses. Choose and write the character trait that best fits the verse.

1. Ephesians 6:1 _____

2. James 4:10 _____

3. Isaiah 54:8 _____

4. Psalm 31:14 _____

5. Nehemiah 8:10 _____

6. Think about which character trait is most lacking in your life. Write two or three sentences telling why you need to develop the trait and how you plan to do so.

_____

_____

_____

_____

OBEDIENCE

The act of doing what I am told with a willing and loving heart

Jesus replied, "All who love me will do what I say. My Father will love them, and we will come and make our home with each of them."
John 14:23

JOY	TRUST	HUMILITY	COMPASSION
BUILDING ON THE ROCK			
Biblical Truth 5	Biblical Truth 6	Biblical Truth 7	Biblical Truth 8
A delight in my life that comes not from my circumstances, but from being in fellowship with God as his child	A complete confidence in God that he will always do everything he promises	An attitude in my heart that I am not better than any other of God's image-bearers	Acts of tenderness and love I give to those who are hurting
I am overwhelmed with joy in the LORD my God! For he has dressed me with the clothing of salvation and draped me in a robe of righteousness. Isaiah 61:10a	But I am trusting you, O LORD, saying, "You are my God!" Psalm 31:14	And all of you, dress yourselves in humility as you relate to one another, for "God opposes the proud but gives grace to the humble." 1 Peter 5:5	Since God chose you to be the holy people he loves, you must clothe yourselves with tenderhearted mercy, kindness, humility, gentleness, and patience. Colossians 3:12
THE WALL OF FELLOWSHIP			
Biblical Truth 1			
THE FOUNDATION OF WISDOM			
THE ROCK			

REVERENCE

An attitude of respect and honor for God

Serve only the LORD your God and fear him alone. Obey his commands, listen to his voice, and cling to him.
Deuteronomy 13:4

HOLINESS	CONFIDENCE	SELF-CONTROL	PEACE
BUILDING ON THE ROCK			
Biblical Truth 9	Biblical Truth 10	Biblical Truth 11	Biblical Truth 12
Purity in my heart in everything I think, say, and do	A strong belief that God will help me do all the things I need to do	An ability to do the right thing even when I don't feel like it	A quietness in my heart because Jesus is with me and has forgiven my sins
The Scriptures say, "You must be holy because I am holy." 1 Peter 1:16	For I can do everything through Christ, who gives me strength. Philippians 4:13	But we belong to the day; so we should control ourselves. 1 Thessalonians 5:8a ICB	And let the peace that comes from Christ rule in your hearts. Colossians 3:15a
THE WALL OF IMAGE-BEARING			
Biblical Truth 2			
THE FOUNDATION OF WISDOM			
THE ROCK			

7. Read the character traits and their verses. Identify which traits are exhibited by the students in the following scenario:

ELLA: A new family moved in next door. I want to invite them to church, but I'm a little nervous.

Devin: I'm sure that God wants you to invite them to church. He will help you be able to speak to them. Why don't you pray about it?

ELLA: You're right. When I pray, God really helps to quiet my heart. He helps me remember that he loves me, has forgiven me, and will help me do what I need to do.

_____

_____

_____

_____

Read the character traits related to servanthood. Write **T** or **F** on the lines.

8. _____ Truthfulness is not important in my thought life because servants don't need to be honest with others.

9. _____ Servanthood requires both friendly and kind attitudes toward others.

10. _____ It is not possible to serve others without having a tender heart toward them and forgiving them whenever it is necessary.

11. _____ There is no reason to be kind-hearted when serving as long as you get the job done.

12. Choose one of the character traits listed. Write a couple of sentences describing how you plan to develop that character trait in your life and why it is important to you.

_____

_____

LOYALTY

Continuing faithfulness in loving and serving God and others

There are "friends" who destroy each other, but a real friend sticks closer than a brother.
Proverbs 18:24

FRIENDLINESS	HONESTY	KINDNESS	FORGIVENESS
BUILDING ON THE ROCK			
Biblical Truth 13	Biblical Truth 14	Biblical Truth 15	Biblical Truth 16
Kind actions, words, and smiles that show others how special they are	Truthfulness in everything I think, say, and do	Loving acts of service and courtesy I give to others	A choice to love those who have been unkind to me
A friend is always loyal, and a brother is born to help in time of need. Proverbs 17:17	Honesty guides good people; dishonesty destroys treacherous people. Proverbs 11:3	See that no one pays back evil for evil, but always try to do good to each other and to all people. 1 Thessalonians 5:15a	Make allowance for each other's faults, and forgive anyone who offends you. Remember, the Lord forgave you, so you must forgive others. Colossians 3:13
THE WALL OF SERVANTHOOD			
Biblical Truth 3			
THE FOUNDATION OF WISDOM			
THE ROCK			

The final wall in the House of Truth is the Stewardship wall. Explain how orderliness, dependability, perseverance, and initiative are important character traits for stewards.

GRATITUDE

Thankfulness in my heart that I express to God and others for the blessings that I receive from them

Give thanks to the Lord, for he is good! His faithful love endures forever.
Psalm 107:1

ORDERLINESS	DEPENDABILITY	PERSEVERANCE	INITIATIVE
BUILDING ON THE ROCK			
Biblical Truth 17	Biblical Truth 18	Biblical Truth 19	Biblical Truth 20
The ability to conduct the activities of my life in an orderly and harmonious way	An ability to complete everything I am responsible for with a willing attitude	An ability to continue fulfilling my responsibilites even when it is hard to do so	An ability to see what needs to be done and do it without being told
But be sure that everything is done properly and in order. 1 Corinthians 14:40	"Be sure to carry out the ministry the Lord gave you." Colossians 4:17	Patient endurance is what you need now, so that you will continue to do God's will. Then you will receive all that he has promised. 1 Thessalonians 5:8a ICB	Whatever you do, do well. Ecclesiastes 9:10a
THE WALL OF STEWARDSHIP			
Biblical Truth 4			
THE FOUNDATION OF WISDOM			
THE ROCK			

13. Orderliness: _____

_____

_____

14. Dependability: _____

_____

_____

15. Perseverance: _____

_____

_____

16. Initiative: _____

_____

_____

Getting Started and Topic 1

1. Write the words to Psalm 86:11. _____

_____

_____

_____

2. Write the definition of truth. _____

_____

3. Read the sentences below. For each sentence, write **T** if it is true or **F** if it is false. Then write whether you used your **senses**, **reasoning**, or **both** to know if the statement is true or false.

	True or False	How I Know
a. An ad shows a successful young man driving a sports car. If you buy the same brand of car, you will be successful too.	_____	_____
b. Three boxes of books weighing four pounds each will weigh a total of 12 pounds.	_____	_____
c. If three boxes of books weigh a total of 12 pounds, four boxes of books will always weigh 16 pounds.	_____	_____
d. If someone does something kind for you, you can know for sure that person likes you.	_____	_____
e. It is very hot outside today.	_____	_____
f. My senses always tell me what is true.	_____	_____
g. If most students in your class believe a certain behavior is correct, then it is correct.	_____	_____
h. My ability to reason will always lead me to the truth.	_____	_____

5.1 Getting Started and Topic 1, continued

Read the sentences below. Based on the definition of truth, explain why the sentence is either **true** or **false**.

4. This photo proves that you can bend a straw by placing it in a glass of water.

This sentence is ____________ because ____________

____

____

____

____

____

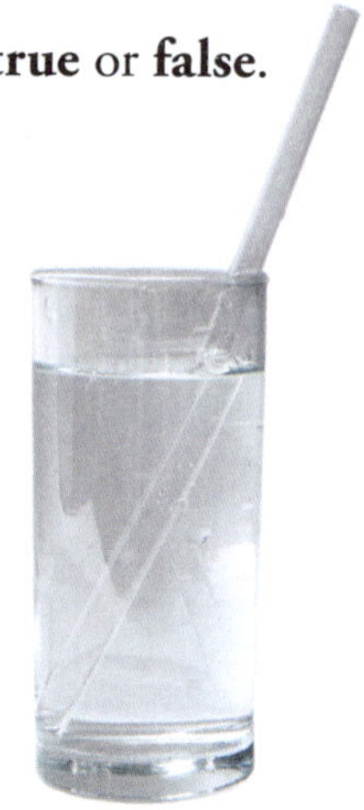

5. In the picture below, there are currently no clouds in the sky, therefore it is not going to rain within the next few minutes.

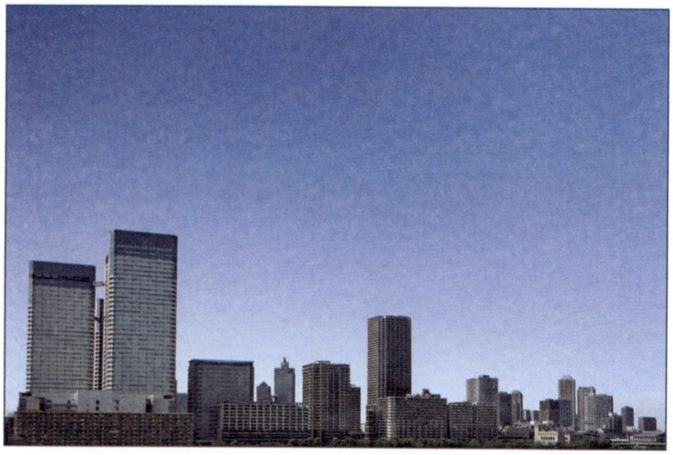

This sentence is ____________

because ____________

____

____

____

____

____

____

6. All worldviews include beliefs related to **truth**, **God**, **the universe**, **people**, and **right and wrong**. Look at the House of Truth model which represents the biblical Christian worldview. Write the corresponding belief next to each part of the House of Truth.

Rock: ____________

____

Foundation: ____________

____

Four walls: ____________

____

____

Roof: ____________

____

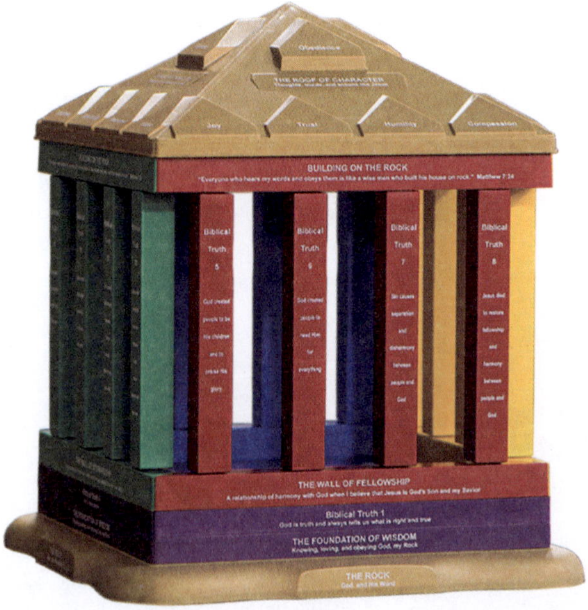

1. What are all the monotheistic religions based upon? _____
_____
_____

2. What are three of the world's major monotheistic religions? _____
_____

3. What does each of the three monotheistic religions believe it possesses? _____
_____

4. Name the book that each monotheistic religion believes is the source for its worldview.

Judaism: _____   Christianity: _____   Islam: _____

5. On what do Jews, Christians, and Muslims agree about the source of truth upon which they base their

religions? _____
_____

6. Each major religion believes God spoke truth through a person. Name three such people.

Judaism: _____   Christianity: _____   Islam: _____

7. If Jews, Christians, and Muslims agree that God spoke truth to them, what do they disagree about?
_____
_____
_____

8. How does God speak truth to us? _____
_____

Write the verse and reference from Topic 2 that explains why each statement is false.

9. Statement: People should be free to follow the "god" of their choice since one person's god may be different from another person's god.

Scripture: _____

_____ Reference: _____

10. Statement: Jesus is one of many ways and many truths that lead to heaven and eternal life.

Scripture: _____

_____

_____ Reference: _____

11. Why did God speak truth to us? _____

_____

_____

_____

12. Each monotheistic religion believes it possesses written truth contained in books available for all to read. The writers mentioned, or cited, in Topic 2 include Isaiah, Jeremiah, John, Matthew, Moses, Muhammad, and Paul. Fill in the names in the diagram below and label each circle to show which writers are associated with each religion.

1. Read the verses. For each verse, identify the truth(s) that God reveals about himself and the things he uses to reveal his truth.

	Scripture	Truth God Reveals	Things God Uses
A.	Job 12:7–10		
B.	Psalm 89:5–8		
C.	Luke 12:23–28		
D.	Psalm 139:13–16		
E.	Psalm 104:24		
F.	Acts 14:17		

2. Which verses teach that everyone can know and understand the truths that God reveals through creation? Circle your answer(s).

a. Psalm 19:1–4   b. Psalm 97:6   c. Job 36:24–25   d. Romans 1:19–20

3. Which of the above verses says we have no excuse for ignorance? _____

4. Many Christian hymn writers have drawn inspiration from nature and the way it proclaims God's glory. One example is the second verse of "Joyful, Joyful, We Adore Thee," as follows:

All Thy works with joy surround Thee,

Earth and heav'n reflect Thy rays,

Stars and angels sing around Thee,

Center of unbroken praise.

Field and forest, vale and mountain,

Flow'ry meadow, flashing sea,

Singing bird and flowing fountain

Call us to rejoice in Thee.

Use the lines below to write a song or poem about how God's existence and his nature are revealed through his creation. _____

_____

_____

_____

_____

_____

_____

_____

_____

_____

5. Write a sentence about what each image tells you about God.

a. _____

_____

_____

b. _____

_____

_____

_____

1. From what Greek word does the word *Bible* come?

_____

What does the Greek word mean? _____

_____

2. Why is the Bible also called *the Scriptures*?

_____

_____

_____

3. If human beings wrote the words of the Bible, why is it called *the Word of God*? _____

_____

_____

_____

4. If human beings wrote the words of the Bible, why is it called *the Truth*? _____

_____

_____

Fill in the blanks in the exercises below.

5. The Old Testament includes _____ books of _____, beginning with Genesis and ending with _____. There are _____ books of _____ in the Old Testament, beginning with _____ and ending with Esther. The next _____ books of the Old Testament are called the books of _____. They begin with the book of _____ and conclude with the Song of Solomon. Finally, there are _____ books of _____ in the Old Testament beginning with _____ and ending with _____. There are _____ books in the Old Testament.

6. The New Testament includes _____ books of _____, beginning with Matthew and ending with _____. There are _____ books of _____ in the New Testament, beginning with _____ and ending with _____. There is only _____ book of _____ in the New Testament. It is called the book of _____. There are _____ books in the New Testament.

7. a. Over how many years was the Bible written before it was complete? _____

   b. About how many people did God choose to write the Bible? _____

8. What word describes how God enabled people to write the Scriptures? _____

9. The Holy Spirit enables people to understand the Scriptures through what? _____

10. The people who wrote the Bible were not like robots, puppets, or machines. Yet everything they wrote was inspired by God. Explain.

_____

_____

_____

_____

Circle the word that best completes the sentence.

11. Most of the Old Testament was written in Hebrew / English / Greek.

12. Most of the New Testament was written in Hebrew / Roman / Greek.

13. Draw lines to match how the Greek and Hebrew languages differ from one another.

- Its alphabet has no vowels.

Greek •

- Its alphabet includes vowels.

Hebrew •

- It reads left to right.

- It reads right to left.

14. Circle the verse that says Scripture is helpful for teaching us what is true, to help us understand what is wrong in our lives, and for God to prepare and equip his people to do every good work.

Psalm 23

1 Corinthians 2:12–13

2 Timothy 3:16–17

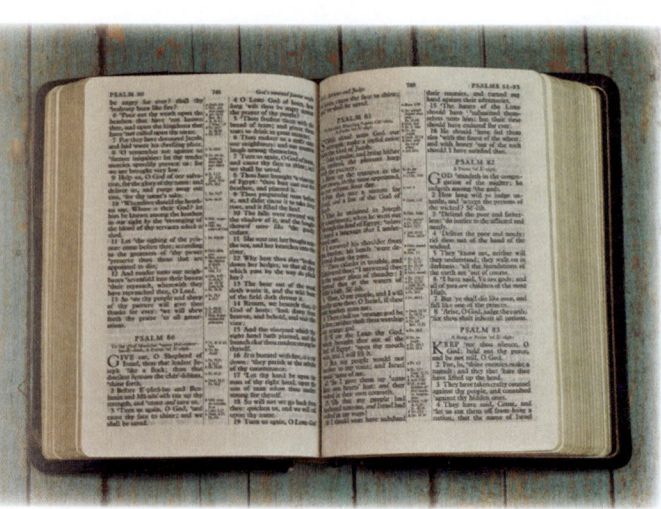

Match each verse to the truth it reveals.

_____ **1.** Romans 1:20

_____ **2.** Colossians 1:16

_____ **3.** Ephesians 1:12

_____ **4.** Romans 5:12

_____ **5.** Genesis 3:15

_____ **6.** Isaiah 53:5

A. God created us to bring him praise and glory.

B. God's invisible qualities—his eternal power and divine nature—are known to us through the universe he created.

C. Sin and death came into the world through one man and now affect all people.

D. God created all things in heaven and on Earth, visible and invisible, and all power and authority.

E. Jesus died for our sins so that he could redeem us from the punishment we deserve.

F. God planned to redeem us through the Child to whom Satan would cause harm, but who would ulitmately destroy Satan.

7. Use a highlighter to show the three ways that God reveals truth to us.

through creation   through newspapers   through television

through the Bible   through Jesus   through advertisements

8. Find and circle the five names for Jesus identified in your Student Textbook.

```
D T A C O S D B W I D Z D V K B S
L P M A T T L M S Y V R V K T Q O
R G G I L Q N I K M E W Z Z H E N
O K O Z F D V D O H T R H Y I C O
W U B L F O N T P N G A W W R N F
E A T W Q B R E A D O F L I F E M
H D U D I J H A T T T F I P B H A
T H Q Z M S G E G D J C J V M Y N
F U D S D O R X I X C O B U D M G
O L D O T U I M L D H L U I D G N
T N O M L V R K T T Q M B Q Y A B
H G D T X C E U Q F V A T X A Z H
G F C Y E S W V A W T U S H E S P
I J F A F J Q U U A Q F Q P R X M
L X K R F K N N H O H U B Q Z K J
```

9. Explain how you know that Jesus was not a ghost when he was on Earth. _____

_____

_____

Jacob's words in Genesis 49:10 promised that Jesus would come from the tribe of Judah. Jesse was one of Judah's descendants. King David was a descendant of Jesse. Read Isaiah 11:1–2. Answer the questions.

10. What image was used in Isaiah to describe David's family?

_____

11. What image was used to describe Jesus? _____

_____

12. According to this verse, what would be special about Jesus?

_____

_____

_____

In Nazareth, Jesus read from the scroll of Isaiah. Read Luke 4:16–18. Write the letter on the blank to match the correct answers.

13. What would Jesus do . . .

_____ for the poor?   A. release them, proclaim liberty or freedom

_____ for the captives?   B. have them see

_____ for the blind?   C. bring good news to them

_____ for the oppressed?   D. set them free, set at liberty

14. What did Jesus affirm was upon him? _____

15. What does John 18:37 say that Jesus came to do? _____

_____

16. Did Jesus do these things? Explain. _____

_____

_____

Topic 5, Part 2 and Topic 6

1. Read the names below. Cross out the ones that are not names for Jesus used in the Bible.

Lion of Judah   The Way   Messenger of Allah   Son of Man   BREAD OF LIFE

Light of the World   Model of Conduct   **The Life**   FIRSTBORN OF ALL CREATION

The Truth   **Word of God**   Good Shepherd   Best of Mankind

Son of God   Redeemer   Prophet of Penitence   **Shoot from the stump of Jesse**

Image of the Invisible God   LORD   **The Reminder**   **Mighty One of Jacob**

2. Which of Jesus' names is your favorite? Why?

_____

_____

_____

_____

_____

Match each verse from Isaiah, in the Old Testament, to the verse in the New Testament where Jesus fulfills it, confirming the truth of God's Word.

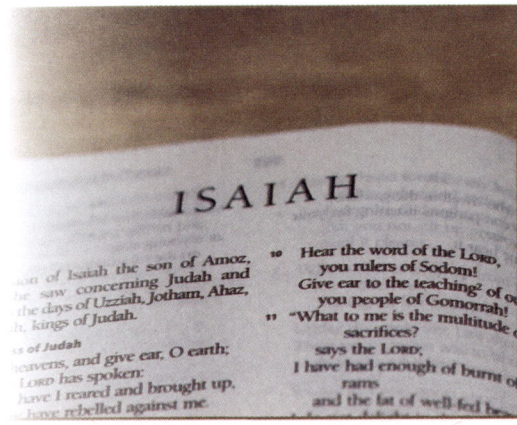

_____ **3.** Isaiah 48:17   A. John 10:14–15

_____ **4.** Isaiah 45:19   B. Revelation 21:5

_____ **5.** Isaiah 35:5–6   C. John 18:37

_____ **6.** Isaiah 53:6   D. Luke 7:22

_____ **7.** Isaiah 65:17   E. John 14:6

8. Refer to Topics 5 and 6. Give an example of a time when Jesus personally revealed . . .

a. the truth of God's words: _____

_____

b. God's compassion for his image-bearers: _____

_____

c. God's plan to redeem all of creation: _____

_____

9. What promise of God does Jesus still have to reveal the truth about in the future?

10. Would you have reacted like Thomas did when he heard the disciples say they had seen Jesus? Why or why not? _____

_____

_____

11. What did Thomas say when he finally saw the risen Jesus?

_____

_____

12. What did Jesus say that people who believe in him without having seen him would be?

_____

Use the Word Bank to answer Exercises 13–15.

13. Circle two ways that we can know about Jesus today.

14. Draw a rectangle around two ways that Jesus described the Holy Spirit.

15. Highlight three things the Holy Spirit does for us in John 14:16–17, 25–26.

16. Where does Jesus promise the Holy Spirit will dwell? _____

17. Write the words to Psalm 86:11. _____

_____

_____

> **Word Bank**
>
> the Spirit of truth
>
> He teaches us.
>
> He reminds us of what Jesus said.
>
> through eyewitness testimony recorded in the Bible
>
> He is with us forever.
>
> through the Holy Spirit
>
> the Helper

18. Jason is not a Christian. "Jesus died a long time ago," says Jason. "You were not alive then. How can you possibly say that you know him?" What would you tell Jason?

_____

_____

_____

_____

_____

Getting Started and Topic 1   6.1

1. a. Write the words of this week's memory verse, Hebrew 11:6, and answer the questions.

_____

_____

_____

   b. What is impossible to do without faith? _____

   c. What does God do for those who seek him? _____

2. Read Romans 1:20 and 2:14–15. Explain how these Scriptures point to evidence that God exists.

_____

_____

_____

_____

_____

_____

3. Read each statement. Make an **X** to identify it as a monotheistic or as a naturalistic (atheistic) worldview.

	Monotheistic	Naturalistic
a. All matter has existed eternally.		
b. The universe's design and order point to a Creator.		
c. Everything that exists was created.		
d. The universe developed through random, accidental events.		

4. God has given people a conscience. People in all cultures and societies know that some things are right and others wrong. Underline those things that are universally considered to be wrong.

stealing   lying   worshipping

MURDERING   abusing a child   eating squid

kidnapping   BEING UNFAITHFUL TO ONE'S HUSBAND OR WIFE

cheating people   failing to vote   wearing red

Not only does the Bible provide evidence of God's existence, it also tells us that we can know him. Read the following Scriptures and answer the questions.

5. Read Jesus' words in John 14:7. What evidence did Jesus give for God's existence?

_____

_____

_____

6. Read Psalm 90:2. What does this verse say about God's existence?

_____

_____

_____

7. Read Psalm 14:1. What does the psalmist say is true of those who deny God's existence?

_____

8. Read Hebrews 11:3. What does this verse say about the existence of the universe?

_____

_____

9. Check the phrases that describe design and order within creation.

_____ the water and rock cycles

_____ the rise and fall of tides

_____ the girls' volleyball team

_____ the seasons of the year

_____ the distance of the earth from the sun

_____ the distance of the moon from Earth

10. Something that exists must have a cause. Explain why this is a true statement and how it can be used to prove the existence of God. _____

_____

_____

_____

Match each term with its definition.

1. _____ Idol

2. _____ Polytheism

3. _____ *Theos*

4. _____ Theism

5. _____ Gentiles

6. _____ Monotheism

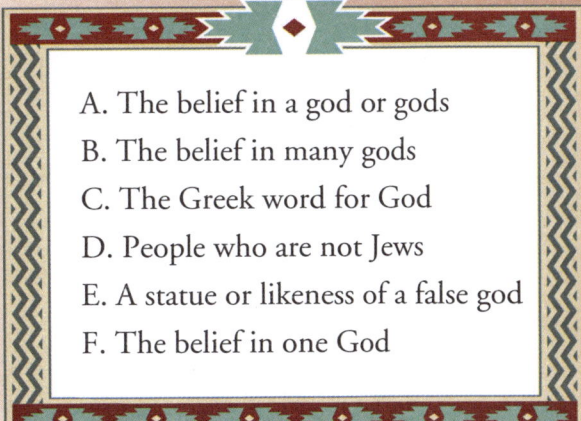

A. The belief in a god or gods
B. The belief in many gods
C. The Greek word for God
D. People who are not Jews
E. A statue or likeness of a false god
F. The belief in one God

Look up the verses and read the statements below. Write **T** for true statements and **F** for false ones.

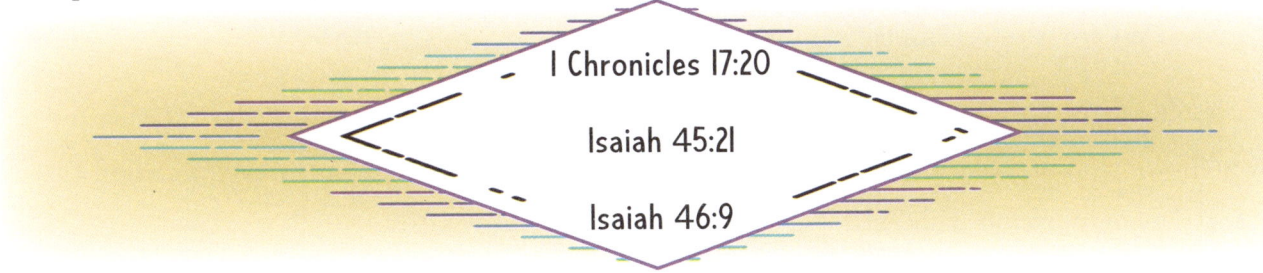

I Chronicles 17:20

Isaiah 45:21

Isaiah 46:9

7. We have listened to God's Word and determined that there is no other God. _____

8. Many gods exist and all have the power to save us from our sins. _____

9. Although God is still the highest god, there are lesser gods who serve him. _____

Read Tia's, Grant's, and Cassie's views of God. Write the type of worldview that each expresses on the lines.

10. **Tia:** I believe in my tribe's view of hundreds of spiritual beings that are central to our religious life. I carve kachinas to represent these spirits.

_____

11. **Grant:** Various gods control the world and can cause floods, fires, and volcanic eruptions unless people offer sacrifices to appease them.

_____

12. **Cassie:** I believe in one, and only one, true God.

_____

An idol is anything we put first before God. Read the sentences below. Underline the word or words that are clues to the fact that the speaker might be worshipping something or someone other than God.

13. I like to keep an open mind. I have read many books on spirituality; I chant regularly; I meditate daily in order to open myself to the divine spirits in nature.

14. The key to life is having plenty of money. I spend lots of time checking on my investments. Staying financially fit is my highest priority. My goal is to retire with over three million dollars.

15. I work out at the gym seven days a week. Fitness is extremely important to my life. I take vitamins, run two or three miles a day, and buy the best running gear I can afford. Church is okay, but I rarely go because the gym is less crowded on Sunday mornings.

16. You should see the number of people who follow me on social media! I have hundreds of friends and a huge following on my blog. Popularity makes me feel good. I don't know what I'd do if I couldn't check my social media accounts daily.

17. I'm totally into dogs! I breed dogs and take them to dog shows. I don't have much time for worship because the shows I enter are often on Sundays. I live for my purebred pups.

18. I play an online warfare-strategy game with my friends. This has got to be the best video game ever! I play until two in the morning most Saturday nights. I'm too tired to go to church, but so what?

What does God say about idolatry? Read the Scriptures and the questions. Fill in the circle in front of the correct answer.

19. Exodus 20:3–5: What did God tell his people that they should never make?
⭘ beautiful carvings for the temple ⭘ stained glass windows ⭘ statues to worship

20. Deuteronomy 4:16–18: What did God forbid?
⭘ making and worshipping figures of animals ⭘ decorations that depict animal life

21. Deuteronomy 4:19: What did God say not to do?
⭘ observing the heavens to determine planting seasons ⭘ worshipping planets and stars

Some people believe that God is an impersonal force, much like the wind, a magnetic field, or an electrical charge. Read the following verses. Write how the verse contradicts the idea of God as a force.

1. Psalm 9:7–8 _____

_____

_____

2. Psalm 14:2 _____

_____

_____

3. Psalm 17:6 _____

_____

4. Hebrews 1:2 _____

_____

5. As a personal Being, God has thoughts. Read the sentences. On the shorter lines, write **T** if the sentence is true and **F** if the sentence is false. Below each sentence, write a verse or part of a verse that helped you decide your answer. Include the Scripture reference.

a. _____ Because God is a personal Being, he thinks in the same way people think.

_____

_____

b. _____ Because God is a personal Being, there is a limit to the things he can think

about. _____

_____

_____

c. _____ Because people are not God, they should abandon the idea of ever

getting to know his thoughts. _____

_____

_____

d. _____ Because God is a personal Being, he has thoughts, but they

are higher than our thoughts. _____

_____

God is a Person. He has both thoughts and feelings. He communicates to people. Match God's communication with the person to whom he spoke. If you are unsure, read the verses before or after those listed.

6. _____ "Build a large boat from cypress wood and waterproof it with tar, inside and out." (Genesis 6:14)

7. _____ "[1]Leave your native country, your relatives, and your father's family, and go to the land that I will show you. [2]I will make you into a great nation. I will bless you and make you famous, and you will be a blessing to others." (Genesis 12:1–2)

8. _____ "Now go, for I am sending you to Pharaoh. You must lead my people Israel out of Egypt." (Exodus 3:10)

A. Isaiah

B. Moses

C. Paul

D. Abraham

E. Noah

F. David

9. _____ Then I heard the Lord asking, "Whom should I send as a messenger to this people? Who will go for us?" I said, "Here I am. Send me." (Isaiah 6:8)

10. _____ [4]He fell to the ground and heard a voice saying to him, "Saul, Saul, why are you persecuting me?" [5]"Who are you, Lord?" Saul asked. And the voice replied, "I am Jesus, the one you are persecuting. [6]Now get up and go into the city, and you will be told what you must do." (Acts 9:4–6)

11. _____ "Your house and your kingdom will continue before me for all time, and your throne will be secure forever." (2 Samuel 7:16).

12. Underline all the trustworthy ways we can learn God's thoughts and plans for our lives.

through our daydreams	through God's Word	through creation
through our choices	through our memories	through Jesus
through our homework	through our complaining	through our mistakes

13. Do you ever wonder what God thinks? Why is setting aside a time for meditating on God's Word a good idea?

_____

_____

_____

_____

_____

_____

Read the verses. On each line, write the emotion that God displays in the verse.

1. Hosea 11:1 _____   **2.** Psalm 86:15 _____

3. Isaiah 5:25 _____   **4.** Isaiah 62:5 _____

5. 1 John 4:9 _____   **6.** Matthew 26:38 _____

7. God feels emotions. He has a will to make choices, and he acts on those choices. Use the Word Bank to complete the flow chart graphic organizer.

Word Bank		
love	angry	chose
rebellion	discipline	sorrow

Before the creation of the world, God _____ to create us.

↓

The sins of the people filled God's heart with _____.

↓

Because of Israel's _____, God became _____.

↓

God used King Nebuchadnezzar to _____ Israel.

↓

God continued to _____ his chosen nation, Israel, as well as all people. He sent Jesus to be the Savior of the world.

As a personal Being, God chooses and acts. Read the verses below. Explain the choice God made.

8. Ephesians 1:3–6 _____

_____

_____

9. Psalm 78:70–71 _____

_____

_____

10. 1 Peter 1:18–20 _____

_____

_____

_____

11. Psalm 89:19–20, 29 _____

_____

_____

_____

12. Deuteronomy 5:1, 7:6–9 _____

_____

_____

God chose the nation, its kings, and the family line through which the Savior would be born. Read the paraphrased verses. Write **Israel**, **the king**, or **the family** according to the content of the verse.

13. _____ Joseph was a descendant of David, which meant he had to go to Bethlehem in Judea, David's family home. He traveled there from the village of Nazareth in Galilee (Luke 2:4).

14. _____ God told Joshua that the time had come for him to lead the Israelites across the Jordan River into the land God was giving them (Joshua 1:2).

15. _____ So there at Hebron, King David made a covenant before the Lord with all the leaders of Israel. And they anointed him king over the entire country (2 Samuel 5:3).

1. God is a perfect, moral Being. What does this mean? _____

_____

_____

2. God is perfect in holiness. What does this mean? _____

_____

_____

3. What does God command his image-bearers to be? Why? _____

_____

_____

4. What does it mean that God is perfect Righteousness? _____

_____

_____

Match the symbol to the attribute of God.

5. _____ The Alpha and Omega; God is eternal.

6. _____ The Trinity; God is Three in One.

7. _____ God is Holy.

8. _____ God is Righteousness.

9. _____ God is Love.

A.    B.    C.

D.    E.

God is perfect Righteousness. Read the passages below. Explain how the righteousness of God is mentioned in each of the verses.

10. Job 36:3 _____

_____

11. Psalm 7:11 _____

_____

Read the paraphrased passages. Choose the nation on which God executed righteous judgment.

12. On that night I will pass through Egypt and put to death every firstborn son and firstborn male animal in the land. This is my judgment against all the gods of Egypt, for I am the Lord! (Exodus 12:12)

○ Babylon ○ Israel ○ Assyria ○ Egypt ○ Rome

13. The Lord gave Jeremiah the prophet this message. . . . This is what the Lord says:
"Tell everyone,
and keep nothing back.
Raise a signal flag to alert the people
that Babylon will soon be destroyed!" (Jeremiah 50:1–2)

○ Babylon ○ Israel ○ Assyria ○ Egypt

14. "Hear this, you priests. Pay attention leaders of Israel. Listen, you members of the royal family. God has judged you because you have led the people away from him by worshipping idols at Mizpah and Tabor" (Hosea 5:1).

○ Babylon ○ Israel ○ Assyria ○ Egypt ○ Rome

15. The Bible declares that all human beings have sinned and fall short of God's glory. How then can God declare Christians not guilty if he is a perfectly holy and righteous judge?

_____

_____

_____

_____

_____

_____

16. God is perfect Love. How does he most clearly demonstrate his love for us?

_____

_____

_____

1. Review the memory verse, Hebrews 11:6. Answer the questions.

a. What is absolutely essential to our belief in God? _____

b. Is it possible to know God? Why? _____

c. What is God's response to those who seek him? _____

You have learned that God is pure and holy. His thoughts are above our thoughts; he is perfectly just and righteous and yet altogether loving. Read the verses below. What attributes of God are mentioned in these verses?

2. Colossians 1:15 _____

3. John 4:24 _____

4. 1 Timothy 6:16 _____

Match each verse to the way God has revealed himself in Scripture.

5. _____ Romans 1:20

6. _____ Mark 1:9–11

7. _____ Exodus 3:1–4

8. _____ Hebrews 1:2

9. _____ Exodus 19:9, 16–19

10. _____ Isaiah 6:8

A. God revealed himself through fire and an audible voice.

B. God's invisible qualities—his eternal power and divine nature—are revealed to us through the universe he created.

C. God revealed himself through a cloud, smoke, an earthquake and an audible voice.

D. God revealed himself through an audible voice and a dove.

E. God revealed himself through his Son.

F. God spoke through an audible voice, asking a question.

11. Explain why knowing Jesus is the best way to know God the Father.

_____

_____

_____

_____

12. Pretend you are a detective looking for clues to God's existence and divine attributes. Because God is invisible, you have to look for other clues about him. What clues do the verses below give you about God?

a. John 14:7–11 _____

_____

_____

b. John 8:42 _____

_____

_____

c. John 1:14, 18 _____

_____

13. We have assurance of Jesus' existence, teachings, miracles, and exact quotations of his words. Read the paraphrased passages below. Underline the key word or words that are the same in each passage.

This report is from an eyewitness who is giving an accurate account.
He is telling the truth so that you may continue to believe. (John 19:35).

[1]Many people have attempted to write accounts about the events of Jesus' life and ministry. [2]They used eyewitness reports from the early disciples that we still possess and share today (Luke 1:1–2).

14. Why is it important that we have factual accounts of Jesus' life and ministry?

_____

_____

_____

Getting Started and Topic 1   **7.1**

1. Write your memory verse and its reference. _____

_____

_____

2. What word in your memory verse is a clue that there is only one true God? Explain why.

_____

_____

In the Getting Started section of your textbook, find a Bible verse that supports each sentence below. Write it out and give its reference.

3. God is one God. _____

_____

_____ Reference: _____

4. The Father is God. _____

_____

_____ Reference: _____

5. The Son is God. _____

_____

_____ Reference: _____

6. The Holy Spirit is God. _____

_____

_____ Reference: _____

7. Below are verses from three hymns. Which one tells about the Trinity? Circle it.

Hark, the herald angels sing:
"Glory to the newborn King!
Peace on earth, and mercy mild,
God and sinners reconciled!"

Away in a manger,
No crib for his bed,
The little Lord Jesus
Laid down his sweet head.

Praise God, from whom all blessings flow,
Praise him, all creatures here below;
Praise him above, ye heavenly host;
Praise Father, Son, and Holy Ghost.

Getting Started and Topic 1, continued

8. Fill in the circle(s) of the word(s) that describe the Persons of God.

◯ polytheistic ◯ atheistic ◯ triune ◯ coequal

9. Look up each verse. Explain how each member of the Trinity is involved.

	Scripture Reference	God the Father	God the Son	God the Holy Spirit
A.	Matthew 3:16–17			
B.	John 14:16–17			
C.	1 Corinthians 12:4–6			
D.	2 Corinthians 13:14			
E.	1 Peter 1:1–2			

10. Sierra and Soraya are friends. Soraya is not a Christian. She thinks that Christians, like Sierra, believe there are three gods. What should Sierra say to her?

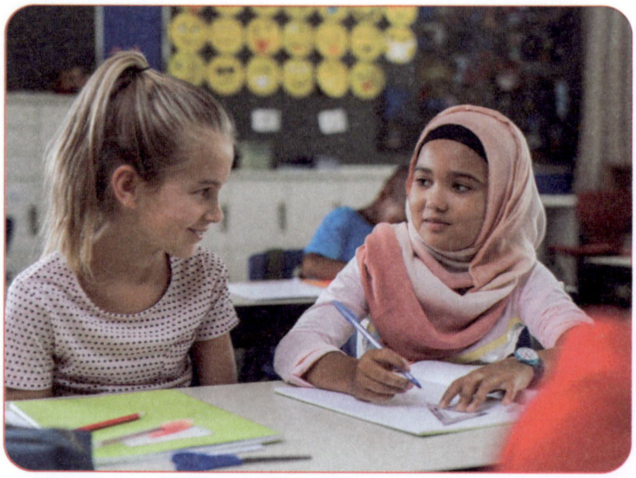

1. In the picture above, Jesus is shown talking to God the Father. Does that mean that Jesus is not God? Write one Bible verse from the Old Testament and one from the New Testment proving your answer.

_____

_____

Read the Bible verses. Match them to the statement.

A. John 5:19   B. Isaiah 7:14   C. John 20:28   D. Jeremiah 3:19

_____ **2.** The prophet is giving God's word to his people, Israel. God chose them as a special people. God was their Father. He wanted the intimate relationship of a father to his children with them.

_____ **3.** When Jesus lived on Earth, he taught the people that he and God the Father are one. Jesus taught them that he was doing his Father's work on Earth as the Father himself had done before sending the Son to Earth. In saying that he was doing his Father's work, Jesus was also saying he was God.

_____ **4.** God spoke these words to Israel through a prophet who told of the birth of God's Son, Jesus, on Earth. This would happen many years in the future. God told the Israelites that the Child would be named "Immanuel," which means "God is with us."

_____ **5.** Thomas did not believe that Jesus was alive again even though the other disciples told him they had seen him. When Thomas finally saw Jesus face-to-face, he declared that Jesus was not only his Lord, but also God.

6. Describe what is happening in the picture to the left. Which verse from the previous page describes the event? _____

_____

_____

_____

_____

_____

7. Read the statements. Mark them with a **T** if they are true or with an **F** if they are false.

_____ a. God chose the Israelites to be his special people and called them his children.

_____ b. The Israelites saw God as their Father and obeyed him without question.

_____ c. Jesus taught he himself is the Father.

_____ d. Jesus called God his own Father.

_____ e. Those who have faith in Christ are adopted as God's children and able to call God Father.

_____ f. The only God is God the Father; Jesus and the Holy Spirit are not God.

_____ g. The name *Immanuel* means *God is with us*.

_____ h. None of the disciples or early Christians believed Jesus was God.

8. Rewrite the false statements so that they are true.

_____

_____

_____

_____

9. Romans 8:15 says that believers cry, "Abba, Father!" The word *abba* is a term expressing affection, like when a baby cries "Daddy!" or "Papa!" Why is it appropriate to use this term for God the Father?

_____

_____

10. In John 20:17, Jesus told Mary Magdalene to go to the apostles and tell them that he was ascending to his Father and their Father, his God and their God. Why is it appropriate to call Jesus your brother?

_____

_____

_____

1. Cross out the pictures that do not relate to what the Holy Spirit was doing at the time of creation in Genesis 1:1–2.

Fill in the circle(s) for the correct answer or answers to each question.

2. Why did King David mention the Holy Spirit in Psalm 51:9–11?

◯ He wanted the anointing of God's Holy Spirit to continue giving him wisdom to rule Israel.

◯ He felt too sinful to be in the presence of God the Holy Spirit.

◯ He said he needed the Holy Spirit to inspire him to write more psalms.

3. In Joel 2:28–29, what did God reveal to the prophet Joel about the Holy Spirit?

◯ The Holy Spirit would be poured out on both male and female servants.

◯ The Holy Spirit would be poured out on both young and old.

◯ The Holy Spirit only comes to prophets.

4. Read Acts 2:1–4 and 16–18. What is the relationship between Joel's prophecy, the day of Pentecost, and the Holy Spirit?

◯ Joel's prophecy about the Holy Spirit was given on the day of Pentecost.

◯ Joel's prophecy about the Holy Spirit was fulfilled on the day of Pentecost.

◯ Pentecost was the day the Holy Spirit chose to show Joel's prophecy was wrong.

5. What did Ananias and Sapphira do in Acts 5:1–11 that was disrespectful to the Holy Spirit?

◯ They sold their property and decided to give some money to the church and keep the rest.

◯ They sold their property and lied about how they distributed the money.

◯ They sold their property and did not give all the money to the apostles.

6. What names did Jesus mention in the command he gave to his disciples in Matthew 28:19?

◯ Peter, James, and John

◯ Father, Son, and Holy Spirit

◯ Abraham, Isaac, and Jacob

7. Place a checkmark by the sentences that correctly use the words eternal or immutable.

_____ a. The minutes the baby cried were eternal.

_____ b. Once the decision was made, it was immutable.

_____ c. The ruins demonstrated how the immutable palace had fallen.

_____ d. People are not eternal because their lives have a beginning.

8. Read Psalm 90:2. How do you know, from this verse,

a. . . . that nothing caused God to exist?

_____

_____

_____

_____

b. . . . that the earth's existence has a cause? _____

_____

_____

c. . . . that the earth is not eternal, as God is? _____

_____

_____

9. Why is a tuning fork a good symbol for God's immutability?

_____

_____

_____

10. Read Psalm 102:24–27. Why is a garment a good contrast to God's immutability? _____

_____

_____

11. Read James 1:17. Why is a shadow a good contrast to God's immutability?

_____

_____

_____

Match each term to its definition.

_____ **1.** Transcendent

_____ **2.** Omniscient

_____ **3.** Omnipresent

_____ **4.** Omnipotent

A. All-powerful

B. Above or beyond the limits of ordinary experience; beyond comprehension

C. All-knowing

D. All-present; present everywhere

5. Explain why the four terms above cannot be applied to human beings.

_____

_____

_____

_____

Write whether the Bible verse describes God as omnipotent, omniscient, or omnipresent.

6. Jeremiah 32:17: _____

7. Psalm 147:5: _____

8. Jeremiah 23:24: _____

9. Matthew 19:26: _____

10. Psalm 139:1: _____

11. Psalm 139:7: _____

12. Write a way in which God is transcendent. _____

_____

_____

_____

13. God is eternal, immutable, omnipotent, omniscient, omnipresent, and transcendent. If you could have just one of these attributes, which would you choose? Why? _____

_____

_____

_____

14. Read the Bible verses. Tell whether the verse identifies a Savior, Creator, Helper, or Teacher. State which Person of the Trinity the verse refers to.

	Bible Verse	Savior, Creator, Helper, or Teacher?	Person of the Trinity
A.	Isaiah 41:10		
B.	Genesis 1:2		
C.	Colossians 1:16		
D.	Hosea 13:4		

15. Underline all the ways that the three Persons of the Trinity work together in unity.

The Trinity works together to teach us.

The Trinity works together to save us.

The Trinity works together to die on the cross for us.

The Trinity works together to sustain creation.

The Trinity works together to help us.

The Trinity works together to baptize us.

The Trinity works together in harmony.

16. Do you think that the Persons of the Trinity could work together in unity if they did not all have the

same attributes? Why or why not? _____

_____

_____

17. Draw a circle around the items that show why the Father deserves thanks and a rectangle around the ones that show why the Son deserves thanks. Underline the items that show why the Holy Spirit deserves thanks. Draw a triangle around the items that apply to all three Persons of the Godhead.

He made us.   He died on the cross.   He helps us understand the Bible.

He answers our prayers.   He baptizes us.   He heals us.   He provides for our needs.

He disciplines us.   He reminds us of what Jesus taught.   He forgives us.

He understands how we feel when we are tempted.   He gave us the Ten Commandments.

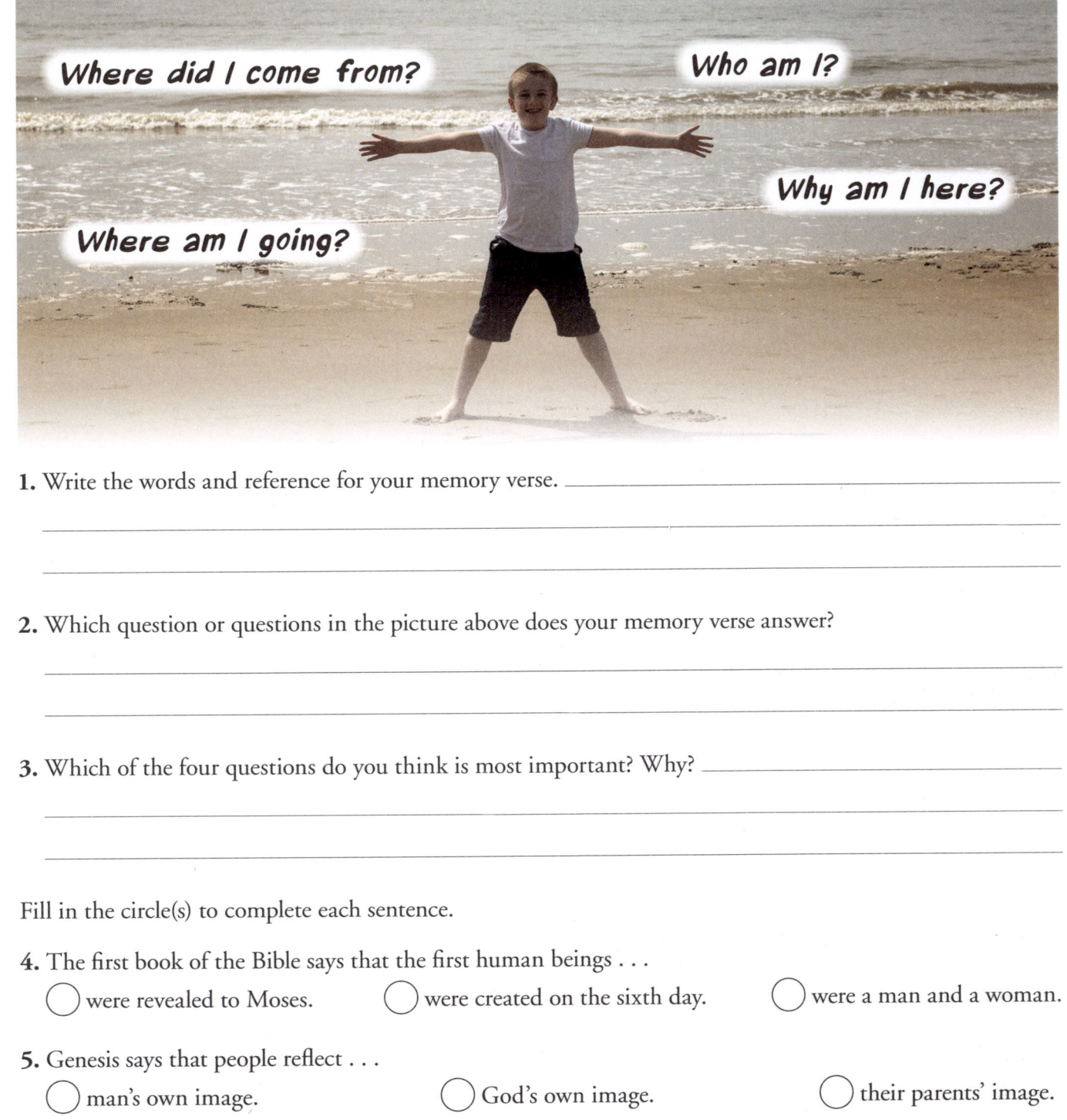

1. Write the words and reference for your memory verse. _____

_____

_____

2. Which question or questions in the picture above does your memory verse answer?

_____

_____

3. Which of the four questions do you think is most important? Why? _____

_____

_____

Fill in the circle(s) to complete each sentence.

4. The first book of the Bible says that the first human beings . . .

◯ were revealed to Moses.   ◯ were created on the sixth day.   ◯ were a man and a woman.

5. Genesis says that people reflect . . .

◯ man's own image.   ◯ God's own image.   ◯ their parents' image.

6. God planned that people would . . .

◯ be born into families.   ◯ multiply the fish of the sea and the birds of the air.

◯ fill the earth.   ◯ have dominion over every living thing.   ◯ subdue one another.

7. Life begins . . .

◯ in your mother's womb.   ◯ with your first breath.   ◯ when you are born.

8. Because God gives life, we must care for each life from the time it begins until death.

a. What are some ways that people show they care about a baby before it is born? _____

_____

b. What are some ways to care for babies once they are born? _____

_____

c. What are some ways to care for elderly people? _____

_____

d. What are some ways to show God that you appreciate being alive? _____

_____

Match the Bible verse to the sentence to prove that the sentence is false. One is used twice.

A. Job 33:4   B. Genesis 1:28   C. Genesis 1:27   D. Acts 17:26   E. Genesis 2:7, 21–22

_____ **9.** People are the result of billions of years of the accidental interaction of eternal cosmic materials.

_____ **10.** God created Adam and Eve together at the same time and in the same way.

_____ **11.** God creates all people on earth the same way he created Adam and Eve.

_____ **12.** God said the earth is too small to provide for the needs of Adam and Eve's descendants.

_____ **13.** As people multiplied, they created nations and decided the borders for their nations and how long their nations would exist.

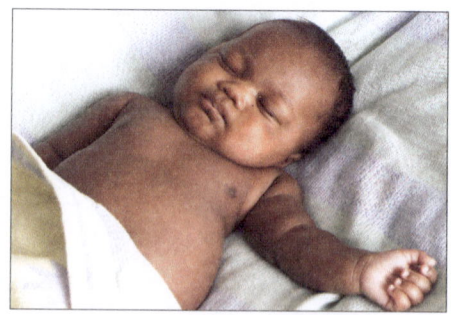

_____ **14.** After God created Adam and Eve and commanded them to fill the earth, he was no longer responsible for the creation of human life.

Match each term to its meaning and to the Bible verse that gives an example of that meaning.

_____, _____ **1.** Moral   A. Able to relate to God   F. Psalm 119:30

_____, _____ **2.** Rational   B. Being able to have feelings   G. Romans 2:15

_____, _____ **3.** Spiritual   C. Knowing right from wrong   H. 1 John 4:19

_____, _____ **4.** Volitional   D. The ability to reason and think   I. Romans 8:16

_____, _____ **5.** Emotional   E. Able to make choices   J. 1 Corinthians 2:16

Read the sentences. Mark them with a **T** for true or an **F** for false.

_____ **6.** God created me with the ability to choose to live according to God's truth and laws.

_____ **7.** My conscience gives me the ability to be awake and aware of my surroundings.

_____ **8.** I can love God because he made me an emotional being.

_____ **9.** Because I am a spiritual being, I am not a physical being.

_____ **10.** Although I sometimes think the wrong things and make mistakes, I am a rational being.

_____ **11.** The Holy Spirit can help me control my thoughts.

_____ **12.** God never experiences anger, grief, or sadness.

_____ **13.** When I volunteer to do something, I show that I am a volitional being.

_____ **14.** A moral person is never tempted to do anything wrong.

15. Rewrite the false sentences so that they are true.

_____

_____

_____

_____

_____

_____

16. A robot can be programmed to make choices. Can we say it is made in God's image? Why or why not? _____

_____

_____

_____

_____

17. Some dogs howl when their owners are gone. Cats hiss when they get angry. Since animals express their feelings, can we say they are made in God's image?

Why or why not? _____

_____

_____

_____

_____

_____

18. Underline the item(s) that the Bible says make people valuable.

fashion sense   worldview   HEIGHT   common sense   intelligence   beauty

wealth   HAVING THE RIGHT FRIENDS   **reading the Bible**   gender

race   athletic ability   sense of humor   going to church   **weight**

national origin   **being good at crafts**   speed   musical talent   religion

FAME   bearing God's image   speaking ability   **good grades**   LUCK   GOOD MANNERS

19. Is everyone equally valuable? Why or why not? _____

_____

_____

_____

_____

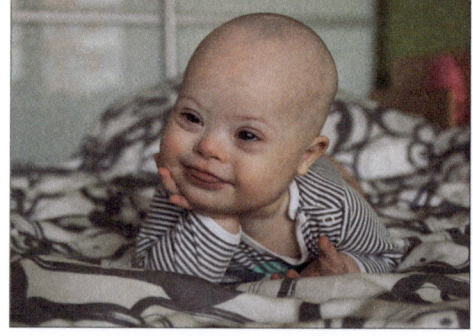

20. Abby does not think that she is smart or pretty. She does not have many friends. She thinks that proves she is not worth very much at all. She is often sad and lonely. What could you tell her to help her feel that she is a worthwhile person?

_____

_____

_____

_____

_____

Read each statement. Use a ✓ to mark whether it is true or false.

	Statement	True	False
1.	The only time you must depend on anyone else to meet your needs is when you are a baby.		
2.	God gives people life, breath, and everything else.		
3.	Your body is a temple and belongs to you alone.		
4.	It is a blessing to depend on God and others to meet our needs.		
5.	God did not create Eve in the same way he created Adam.		
6.	God created the family to be any two or more people who decide to live together.		
7.	Throughout history, people have created nations when and where they were needed.		

8. Explain why each false statement is false.

_____

_____

_____

_____

_____

_____

9. What is the temple of the Holy Spirit? Fill in the circle(s).

○ the universe   ○ every believer's body   ○ a church building
○ the Bible   ○ the garden of Eden   ○ the family and nation
○ a dove   ○ the tabernacle   ○ Jesus' tomb

Match each statement to the Bible verse that proves it is false.

_____ **10.** Nobody owns me. I'm my own boss.

_____ **11.** I don't need to depend on anyone for anything.

_____ **12.** It's my own body. I can treat it any way I want to.

_____ **13.** There's no one I can depend on for my needs.

_____ **14.** I am just fine on my own. I don't need help.

_____ **15.** God said married adults should keep living with their parents.

_____ **16.** Families have no purpose.

_____ **17.** Noah's sons had no descendants.

A. Genesis 2:18

B. Deuteronomy 10:14

C. Genesis 2:24

D. Philippians 4:19

E. Genesis 1:28

F. Job 12:10

G. Genesis 10:32

H. 1 Corinthians 6:19–20

18. Read the two definitions of the word *family*. Compare and contrast the two definitions.

_____

_____

_____

_____

19. What is the difference between a family and a nation?

_____

_____

_____

20. Write a prayer for your family and nation.

_____

_____

_____

_____

_____

_____

_____

_____

Read Romans 7:19–25 to find statements that reveal Paul's image-bearing characteristics.

1. What did Paul say that reveals he is a volitional being and a moral being?

_____

_____

_____

2. What did Paul say that reveals he is an emotional being? _____

_____

_____

3. What did Paul say that reveals he is a rational being? _____

_____

_____

4. Find and write a verse in Lesson 8 that Paul wrote that reveals we are spiritual beings.

_____

_____

5. Use the key to decode the message.

6. Why do you think that we do not like to admit that we are sinners and need the Savior?

_____

_____

_____

7. Read each statement. What image-bearing characteristic does it reflect? Does the statement betray a sinful attitude? Sort the statements and complete the table. There should be one statement within each cell.

I spend time with God.   I want my own way.   I study before my tests.

I am honest when I make a mistake.   I lie when it suits me.

I choose to please God.   I hate certain people.   I never bother with prayer.

I never study because I know it all already.   I express my feelings gently when I am sad or mad.

Characteristic	A positive choice is . . .	A sinful choice is . . .
Volitional		
Moral		
Emotional		
Rational		
Spiritual		

8. Because everyone sins, Isaiah compared people to sheep who go astray. Read Isaiah 40:11, John 10:14–15, and 1 Peter 2:24–25. Describe God's response to his sinful

people. _____

_____

_____

_____

_____

_____

_____

Getting Started and Topic 1

1. Write your memory verse and its reference. _____

_____

_____

2. Circle the four worldview questions that everyone asks about themselves.

Where am I going?   What am I doing?   Where did I come from?

What will I be when I grow up? Why am I here?   Who am I?

What's in it for me?   Who called me last night?   When will I die?

Use the Word Bank to fill in the blanks.

Word Bank
existence   pleasure   eternal   children   sinners   need

3. People who ask why they are on earth have questions about their _____.

4. God is _____, triune, and has never been alone.

5. God does not _____ human beings in order to be happy.

6. God made us for his _____.

7. While we were still _____, Christ died for us.

8. Jesus' death on the cross allows us to be adopted as God's _____.

9. Journalists often employ the "Five Ws and one H" technique to write good news pieces. The five Ws are *who, what, when, where,* and *why.* The H is *how.* Pretend that you are a news reporter writing about God's plan for the creation and redemption of humankind. Respond to the questions that use the four Ws and the H.

Who made us? **Who** redeemed us? _____

_____

What is redemption? _____

_____

When did God plan for our redemption? _____

_____

Why did he do this? _____

_____

How are we saved? _____

_____

10. Janis and Tyler were arguing about why they were created. Read their arguments and check whether you agree or disagree. State your reasons, including a Scripture reference, if possible.

Tyler: I think God made us because he was lonely. After all, the universe is vast and empty. He probably needed someone to talk to.

_____ agree   _____ disagree

_____

_____

Janis: I think God made us because he wanted to share his love with people.

_____ agree   _____ disagree

_____

_____

Tyler: I'm sure that God created the earth for our pleasure. He planned to make people even before he created other creatures.

_____ agree   _____ disagree

_____

_____

Janis: God probably made us as an afterthought. He had no reason to make us or to send Jesus to die for us.

_____ agree   _____ disagree

_____

_____

Tyler: God made people because it pleased him to make us. He sent Jesus to die for us.

_____ agree   _____ disagree

_____

_____

Janis: God sent Jesus to die for us, but that was only after people repented and began to obey his commands.

_____ agree   _____ disagree

_____

Read the verses. Match the verse with the ways to glorify God.

1. _____ We glorify God when we praise and worship him and honor his glory.

2. _____ We glorify God when we tell others about his glory and his wonderful deeds.

3. _____ We glorify God when we suffer persecution for following him.

4. _____ We glorify God when we care for our bodies.

5. _____ We can glorify God in everything we do that is right.

6. _____ We glorify God when we do good works.

> A. 1 Corinthians 6:20
>
> B. Psalm 96:3
>
> C. 1 Peter 2:12
>
> D. Psalm 86:12
>
> E. 1 Peter 4:16
>
> F. James 3:13

7. The words "whatever you do," in 1 Corinthians 10:31, mean that there is no right and good thing you can do that won't glorify God. This includes playing, studying, and doing chores around the house. There is nothing you do that is so ordinary it can't be done for God's glory. You honor God by your humble attitude as you complete your daily tasks, trusting God to help you in all that you do. Underline the things that you do routinely at school or at home.

take out the trash   help a younger sibling   care for a pet   pray

read a devotional book   make dinner   sing in a choir or praise team

study for a test in school   assist your Sunday school teacher   CLEAN YOUR ROOM

fold laundry   coach or teach younger children   give an offering

encourage friends   help a neighbor   invite friends to church

8. We glorify God through our worship. What part of the worship service at church or at school chapel is your favorite? How do you bring glory to God by participation in worship?

_____

_____

9. We glorify God in our family. What do you do or can you do to glorify him in your home?

_____

_____

10. Use the Word Bank to complete the definition of God's glory. Some words will not be used.

Word Bank						
love	excellence	honor	compared	perfect	remarkable	joy

God's _____ _____, majesty,

_____, and greatness that cannot be _____ to

anything else.

11. Use the Word Bank to complete the definition of to glorify God. Some words will not be used.

Word Bank					
declare	honor	attitude	thanksgiving	respect	glory

To _____ God's _____ and to

_____ him with praise and _____ in

every _____ and action.

Consider the four relationships of creation: our relationship with God, within ourselves, with others, and with the earth. Answer the questions.

12. How can you glorify God in your relationship with him?

_____

_____

_____

13. How can you glorify God in your relationship within your own heart through personal examination, reflection, and repentance? _____

_____

_____

14. How can you glorify God in your relationships with others? _____

_____

15. How can you glorify God in your relationship with nature? _____

_____

1. Because we bear God's image, we are relational beings. God created us to need each other and to work together to fill and subdue the earth, ruling over every living creature. Place a check mark in front of each service that you or other people cannot do alone.

_____ build bridges and dam rivers in order to subdue the earth

_____ create and maintain sanctuaries for endangered species

_____ create and enforce fair laws to govern our nation

_____ care for 26 young children in the church nursery while parents worship

_____ worship and revere God as our Creator

_____ responsibly maintain national forests

2. List four ways that you plan to let your light shine before others so that they can see your good works.

a. _____

b. _____

c. _____

d. _____

3. Read the scenarios below. Identify the way in which the student is glorifying God.

a. Tyler always tells the truth. When he was the last player to touch the basketball before it went out of bounds, he raised his hand to let the referee know to give the ball to the other team.

_____

_____

b. Amare reads stories to little children at the public library. She isn't paid to do it; it's a volunteer job.

_____

_____

c. Candace sings in the middle school worship team.

_____

_____

d. Jon's great-grandmother is 90 years old. He visits her in the nursing home and listens to her stories even though she tells the same stories every time Jon visits.

_____

_____

Match each statement about serving others to the Bible reference that describes it.

4. _____ We give up, or lay down, our selfish lifestyles in service to others.

5. _____ We work together in teams so that we might accomplish more.

6. _____ We love our enemies, do good, and lend, expecting nothing in return.

7. _____ We see people in need and help supply their needs.

> A. Ecclesiastes 4:9–12
> B. John 15:13
> C. 1 John 3:17
> D. Luke 6:35–36

Jesus served others. Read the verses and underline the different titles of Jesus in each verse.

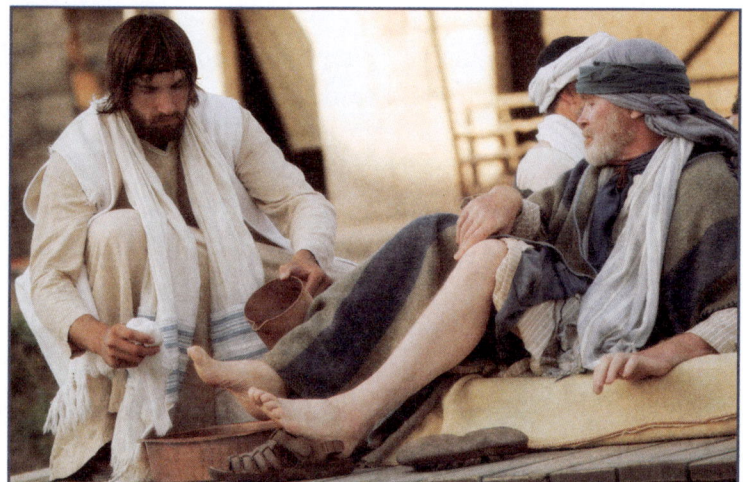

8. The next day John the Baptist saw Jesus coming toward him and said, "Look! The Lamb of God, who takes away the sin of the world!" (John 1:29)

9. You will be like a fresh batch of dough made without the yeast of sin, which is what you really are. Christ, our Passover Lamb, has been sacrificed for us (1 Corinthians 5:7).

10. Jesus is the kind of high priest we need because he is holy and blameless, unstained by sin. He has been set apart from sinners and has been given the highest place of honor in heaven (Hebrews 7:26).

11. Though Jesus was God, he did not think of equality with God as something to grab onto. Instead, he gave up his divine privileges; he took the humble position of a slave (Philippians 2:6–7).

12. "In a burst of anger, I turned my face away from you for a little while. But with everlasting love I will have compassion on you," says the Lord, your Redeemer (Isaiah 54:8).

13. Jesus said, "I am the good shepherd. The good shepherd sacrifices his life for his sheep" (John 10:11).

1. Read John 11:25–26 and write the words here: _____

_____

_____

2. Jesus spoke the words that you just read. He was speaking to Martha, whose brother, Lazarus, had just died. Why would Jesus' words have comforted Martha? Why do they comfort all Christians?

_____

_____

3. What is the biblical worldview answer to the question "Where am I going?"

_____

_____

_____

4. How would someone with an atheistic or naturalistic worldview answer the question "Where am I going?"

_____

_____

_____

5. How would someone with a new spirituality worldview answer the question "Where am I going?"

_____

_____

6. How would a Christian confidently answer the question "Where am I going?" What gives Christians assurance of their eternal destination? _____

_____

7. Read John 3:16 and Ephesians 2:8. Underline the words below that the verses indicate are necessary for eternal life.

| pets | tolerance | belief | compassion | payment | grace |
| luck | fear | respect | study | wisdom | obedience |

8. Jesus' words in John 11:25–26 seem to be contradictions. Fill in the circles in front of the sentences that show the joyful contradictions of the Christian life.

○ Whoever lives in Christ shall never die.   ○ Death is swallowed up in victory.

○ Dying bodies will be replaced by living ones.   ○ Life is sad and eternally painful.

○ Death is the end of life forever.   ○ Let the evildoer still do evil.

9. The apostle John spent the last days of his earthly life on the Greek island of Patmos. There the Lord revealed to him the holy city, the new Jerusalem where Christians will live with him forever. Read Revelation 22:1–3. List five things that will be present in the new Jerusalem.

a. _____

b. _____

c. _____

d. _____

e. _____

10. Read Revelation 22:15. Who won't be in the new Jerusalem? List five types of people who will not enter the city.

_____   _____

_____   _____

_____

11. What does Jesus mean when he says that whoever hears his word and believes in God the Father, who sent him, has eternal life and will not be condemned?

_____

_____

_____

_____

_____

12. What does Jesus mean when he says that all those who have done evil will rise to be condemned?

_____

_____

_____

13. Think of someone who is unsure of his or her eternal destination. How could you help that person come to know Christ as his or her Savior? _____

_____

_____

_____

_____

Fill in the circle(s) that answer the questions.

1. What do naturalists say about the universe?
- ○ The universe does not exist.
- ○ The universe came into being by itself out of nothing.
- ○ The universe has always existed.
- ○ The universe was created.

2. What do Christians say about the universe?
- ○ God created the universe.
- ○ God and the universe have always existed.
- ○ God was created by the universe.
- ○ God and the universe are the same thing.

3. Which explanation did naturalists make that scientist Carl Sagan rejected? Why?

_____

_____

4. Carl Sagan said, "The cosmos is all there is, or ever was, or ever will be."
  a. What does this statement suggest about God?

  _____

  _____

  _____

  b. What does this statement imply that people can know?

  _____

  _____

  _____

  c. Is Sagan correct? Why or why not? _____

  _____

  _____

  _____

  _____

  _____

5. Write whether each sentence is **true** or **false**. Find a Bible verse from Topic 1 in your Student Textbook that proves your answer is correct. Write its reference.

	Sentence	True or False	Reference
A.	Jesus did not exist until he was born on Earth; only God the Father existed when the universe began.		
B.	Jesus is a created being.		
C.	Jesus created everything in the universe.		
D.	God created the universe but other thrones, dominions, rulers, and authorities were already in existence.		
E.	God only created things we can see with our eyes.		
F.	Some things came into existence by themselves.		
G.	Like an artist who uses art supplies to create a painting, God created the universe by using materials that have always existed.		
H.	To understand that the universe was created by the word of God, we need faith.		

6. Rewrite the false sentences from the table above so that they are true.

_____

_____

_____

_____

_____

_____

_____

7. Write your memory verse and its reference. _____

_____

_____

1. What is something you have made or created? _____

_____

2. Why did you create it? Check all the reasons that apply.

☐ as an assignment for school   ☐ as a gift   ☐ to express myself or be creative

☐ because I could   ☐ to solve a problem or meet a need   ☐ to own it   ☐ for fun

Match each Bible verse with the letter that gives the reason why God created the universe.

A. God created the universe because it pleased him.

B. God created the universe for himself.

C. God created the universe to reveal his existence and to show us what he is like.

D. God created the earth to be the home for his image-bearers.

____   **3.** Romans 1:20   ____   **4.** Psalm 104:24   ____   **5.** Genesis 1:28   ____   **6.** Acts 14:17

____   **7.** Psalm 50:10–11   ____   **8.** Revelation 4:11   ____   **9.** Psalm 115:16   ____   **10.** Revelation 21:3

Read Psalm 19:1–4 in your Student Textbook and answer each question according to the words of the psalm. Fill in the circle(s) that apply.

11. What do the heavens and the skies proclaim?

○ God's passion   ○ God's glory   ○ God's craftmanship   ○ God's emotions

12. When do the skies and the heavens tell us about God's creation?

○ day after day   ○ only in the afternoon   ○ night after night   ○ just at sunset

13. What do the heavens and skies speak without?

○ a sound or word   ○ psalms and poems   ○ stories and legends   ○ wisdom

14. Although the heavens and skies do not speak as we do, what do they reveal about God?

○ They make him known.   ○ They tell of his creativity.   ○ They remind us of sin.

15. God owns the earth, and we are stewards of it, but one day, God will create a new earth. Answer the questions.

a. How should you treat the earth as a caretaker of it? _____

_____

_____

b. How will the new earth be different from Earth as it is now? _____

_____

_____

16. God's existence and some of his attributes are made known through creation. Below each picture, write a word to express what that image tells you about God.

_____   _____   _____

Refer to Topic 3 in your Student Textbook. Write your answers on the blank lines. Add the Scripture reference that helped you determine your answer.

1. Carl Sagan believed that the universe sustains itself. How does the biblical Christian worldview of the universe differ from Sagan's belief?

_____

_____

_____ Reference: _____

2. Why have people been able to build and launch space stations, design and build bridges, and develop many areas of modern science that help us rule over and

care for God's earth? _____

_____

_____

_____ Reference: _____

3. What do we mean when we say that God is not limited by the laws he created?

_____

_____

_____ Reference: _____

4. At Jesus' crucifixion, how did God demonstrate that he is not limited by the laws he created for the universe and that Jesus is his Son? _____

_____

_____

_____ Reference: _____

Fill in the circle(s) for your answer.

5. What does God the Father's demonstration at the time of Jesus' death show?

◯ his omnipresence   ◯ his omnipotence   ◯ his invisible nature   ◯ his omniscience

6. What is a miracle?

◯ God's action outside his laws of nature   ◯ God's action at any time and place

Match each Bible verse to what it reveals about the different ways God sustains his creation.

_____ **7.** Psalm 104:5   A. God created and sustains the earth's seasons.

_____ **8.** Genesis 1:24   B. God created and sustains the earth's plants.

_____ **9.** John 5:24   C. God created and sustains the earth's animals.

_____ **10.** Psalm 147:8   D. God created and sustains the earth in space.

_____ **11.** Isaiah 46:4   E. God created and sustains his image-bearers even after death.

_____ **12.** Genesis 8:22   F. God created and sustains his image-bearers even as they age.

13. Complete the crossword puzzle.

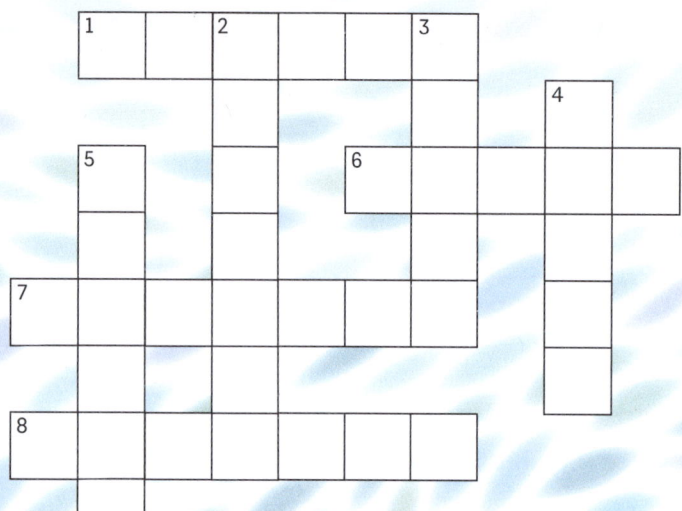

Across
1   Some animals feed on these.
6   This is something creation reveals God has.
7   This happens when God acts outside the laws of nature.
8   There are four of them.
10 This is what God does for everything in creation.
11 This is what God established for the creation to operate.

Down
2   They are tame or wild.
3   This is where land meets water.
4   In him all things hold together.
5   This is also called *the cosmos*.
9   They are image-bearers.
10 Their light reaches Earth.

Topics 4 and 5 `10.4`

1. Cross out the images that do not directly relate to the responsibilities given in Genesis 1:28.

A.

B.

C.

D.

E.

F.

G.

H.

I.

J.

K.

L.

2. Match the images that you did not cross out to the responsibilities listed below.

    a. Fill the earth with people. _____

    b. Subdue the earth. _____

    c. Have dominion over every living creature. _____

3. For each responsibility listed above, give an example of how to carry out it out in a God-honoring way, and an example of what not to do.

	What To Do	**What Not To Do**
A.		
B.		
C.		

4. How did King David respond to God's giving human beings authority over

creation? _____

_____

_____

5. What is a steward? _____

_____

_____

Mark the sentences below **T** for true or **F** for false.

_____ **6.** God's plan for all eternity has been for us to live in eternal harmony with ourselves, each other, and the earth.

_____ **7.** Adam and Eve began to die physically as soon as they were created.

_____ **8.** Moses recorded God's words to Adam and Eve.

_____ **9.** In speaking to Satan, God revealed his plan to redeem and restore harmony in creation through Jesus.

_____ **10.** Only human beings will be set free from death and decay.

_____ **11.** Peter confirmed Isaiah's words that God would create new heavens and a new earth.

_____ **12.** John recorded his vision of the Holy City, the New Jerusalem, in the book of Revelation.

13. Rewrite the false sentences so that they are true.

_____

_____

_____

14. What will the new heavens and new earth and God's redeemed

image-bearers never again experience? _____

_____

_____

15. For what purpose will God create new heavens and a new earth?

_____

_____

1. Write the words for 1 Peter 1:14–16. _____

_____

_____

_____

_____

Read each statement and determine to which category each belongs.

	Moral Awareness	Moral Values
2. An inner knowledge all people possess		
3. Behaviors that are right and good		
4. Behaviors that are valuable for our lives		

5. Read Romans 2:12–15. Answer the questions.
   a. How do those people who have never learned God's law know how to behave righteously?

   _____

   b. For those who do not have the Bible, where has God written his law? _____

   _____

   c. Does your conscience ever accuse you of doing wrong? _____

   d. Does your conscience commend you when you do what is right? _____

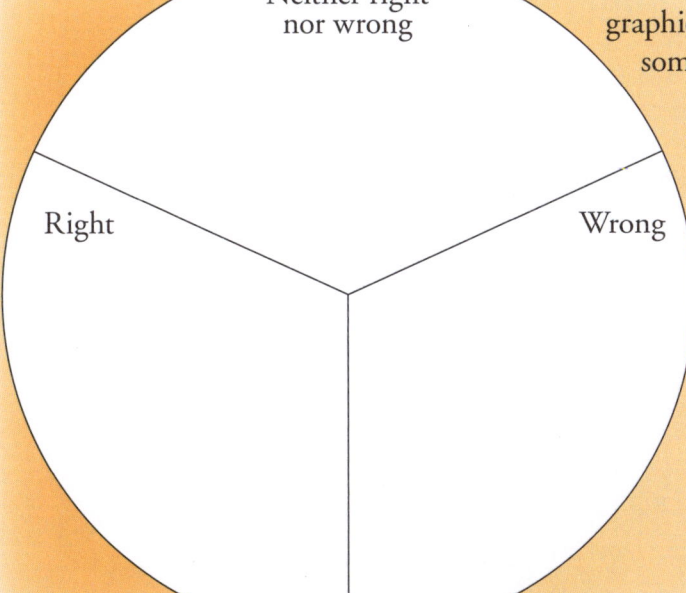

6. Write the letter of the statement into the correct area of the graphic organizer based on whether the statement shows something right, wrong, or neither right nor wrong.

   A. It's okay to tell an insulting joke as long as it's funny.

   B. You should consider others' feelings before saying something that could hurt them.

   C. I can choose what to wear to school.

   D. Cruel teasing and putting people down is no big deal.

Match the description of God's Word or his Law with the correct verse.

7. _____ A lamp to my feet   A. Psalm 19:7

8. _____ A tool to correct us and
                    teach us   B. Psalm 19:8

9. _____ Giving insight for living   C. 2 Timothy 3:16

10. _____ Perfect; a reviving and
                     refreshment for the soul   D. Psalm 12:6

11. _____ Pure; like silver refined
                     in a furnace, purified
                     seven times over   E. Psalm 119:105

12. Read 1 John 2:14. Answer the questions.

    a. Where does God's Word live in us as Christians? _____

    b. Who or what does God's Word help us overcome or defeat? _____

13. Read Psalm 119:9–11. Answer the questions.

    a. How can a young person keep his or her life pure? _____

    _____

    b. Is it important to know God's Word so well you "store" it in your heart? Should you memorize God's

    Word? Why or why not? _____

    _____

    _____

    _____

14. According to 2 Timothy 3:16–17, God's Word influences our moral awareness and our actions in at
    least five ways. List these five influences and purposes of God's written Word.

    a. _____

    b. _____

    c. _____

    d. _____

    e. _____

Nadia has some questions about God's moral laws. Choose the best response to her questions from your reading and fill in the circle.

1. If God has placed a conscience into each person, why do we need to read the Bible?

  ○ Our conscience is good enough to tell us when we do wrong. ○ Our conscience is marred by sin.

  ○ Our conscience only tells when we do what is right. ○ Our conscience just makes us feel guilty.

2. Does the Bible actually tell us what is wrong or right?

  ○ Yes. The Bible shows us the right and wrong way to live. ○ No. The Bible is a history book.

  ○ No. The Bible gives us ideas but not truths. ○ No. Our conscience does that.

God's moral laws are based on his own perfect, moral nature. What do the following Scriptures say about God's moral laws?

3. Psalm 19:7 _____

4. Psalm 119:1 _____

5. Jeremiah 31:33 _____

There are four characteristics of God's moral laws. Write the number of the characteristic next to the sentence that best describes it. Some characteristics will be used more than once.

> **1.** God's moral laws are based on the perfect moral nature of God himself.
> **2.** God's moral laws are objective.
> **3.** God's moral laws are absolute.
> **4.** God's moral laws are universal.

6. _____ God's laws are right and true regardless of what someone may think, believe, or feel.

7. _____ God's laws are flawless and based on his love for us.

8. _____ God's laws apply to all people wherever they live.

9. _____ God's laws are pure and unchanging through all time.

10. _____ God's laws are righteous even if someone disagrees.

11. _____ God's laws are just as true for people in China as they are for people in the United States of America.

Determine if the laws below are universal or absolute, or both. Mark an **X** in the correct column(s).

	Absolute	Universal
12. No one may murder anyone else.		
13. The speed limit is 55 miles per hour.		
14. No one may take another person's property.		
15. No one may legally enslave another person.		
16. Do not throw litter on the highway.		
17. Citizens over age 18 must vote.		
18. No one may eat the meat of animals.		
19. Lying is wrong.		

LEGAL →
← ILLEGAL

Think about the following scenarios and write your ideas about what might happen next.

20. Two countries, A and B, are adjacent and share a border. People in Country A believe that God's laws against murder, lying, and stealing are right and should be enforced, but people from Country B don't believe these laws apply to them. What might happen next? _____

_____

_____

21. Students in Mr. Foster's class can decide on their own classroom rules. Juan thinks a quiet study time is best, but Amelia likes to chat with her neighbors. Since Mr. Foster lets the students do as they please, he never stops Amelia from talking. What might happen next? _____

_____

_____

22. Why is it important that God's laws are universal, absolute, and unchanging?

_____

_____

_____

1. Read 1 Peter 1:14–16. Underline the correct words.

Our conduct is to be (holy, friendly) because God is (good, holy).

By following God's (daily, moral) laws, we no longer live in

ignorance, but in (obedience, relationship) to God.

The Ten Commandments are God's moral laws about our relationship with God and with others. Write the number of the commandment to which each statement refers.

2. _____ We violate God's law when we disobey our parents.

3. _____ We violate God's law when we greedily desire something that is not ours.

4. _____ We violate God's law when we steal the property or ideas of another person.

5. _____ We violate God's law when we are unfaithful to our husband or wife, or we fail to maintain sexual purity reserved for marriage.

6. _____ We violate God's law when we spread rumors, lie under oath, or speak untruthfully about someone else.

7. _____ We violate God's law when we don't attend worship services or set aside time to rest and worship God.

8. _____ We violate God's law when we use God's name to curse, swear, or lie.

9. _____ We violate God's law when something in our life is more important to us than he is.

10. _____ We violate God's law when we take another person's life.

11. _____ We violate God's law when we have idols.

Read Matthew 22:37–40. Write the two greatest commandments on which all the others are based.

12. _____

_____

13. _____

_____

Jesus teaches us that all God's moral laws are based on the two laws that you just wrote.

Read each statement and explain why each is false. Find the Bible verse in Topic 3 that helped you with your explanation.

14. It's okay to hate someone; just don't murder him or her.

_____

_____

_____

Reference: _____

15. It's okay to desire someone else's husband or wife; just don't commit adultery.

_____

_____

_____

Reference: _____

Read each of the scenarios below. Consider whether the person in the story is close to following God's moral law or far from it. A mark near the number nine is very close, or perfectly following God's law. A mark farther from the center shows the person is farther away from God's will. Mark each target as needed.

16. My brother has a new video game that he won't let me play. I'll just play it when he is asleep. He will never know the difference.

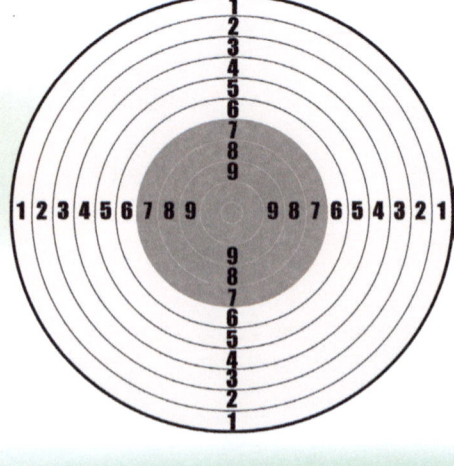

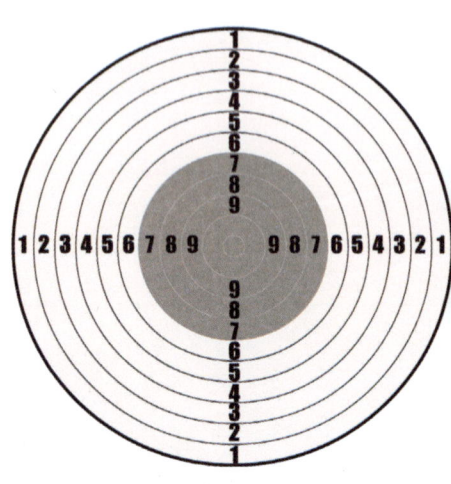

17. I used to have a best friend, but now she is hanging out with other girls. My feelings are hurt, and I'm jealous. I think I'll post a few lies about her on a social media website. That will show her!

Because the Spirit teaches us God's moral law in Scripture and through our conscience, we are responsible for making right choices. Read the statements and consider the choices that could be made. Choose a biblical choice to solve the dilemma.

1. Joshua's mom wants him to help her with the laundry, but his friend wants him to play basketball.
   - ○ He can play basketball and then help his mom if there's still time.
   - ○ He can help his mother first and play basketball later.
   - ○ He can play basketball and tell his mother that she can handle the laundry by herself.

2. Anita went online and read a post that contained several false rumors about a friend.
   - ○ She can pretend that she doesn't know anything about the rumors.
   - ○ She can decide that false rumors are no big deal.
   - ○ She can stand up for her friend and ask that the false rumors be removed from the post.

3. Tamara, an emergency room nurse, has to work every other Sunday and can't attend church.
   - ○ She can attend church midweek or on the Sundays she has off.
   - ○ She can decide that church is not important.
   - ○ She can sleep in on the Sundays she has off.

All God's words are living because they speak to us. Match each verse to its description.

| A. 2 Samuel 22:31 |
| B. Proverbs 6:23 |
| C. Psalm 33:4 |
| D. Ephesians 6:17 |
| E. Hebrews 4:12 |
| F. Isaiah 40:8 |
| G. Psalm 19:7 |

4. _____ God's living Word endures or stands for all time.

5. _____ God's living Word is perfect and trustworthy.

6. _____ God's living Word is proven to be true and his way is perfect.

7. _____ God's living Word is sharper than any sword.

8. _____ God's living Word is a light.

9. _____ God's living Word holds true.

10. _____ God's living Word is the sword of the Spirit.

11. Read Hebrews 4:12. How does God's Word influence our lives?

_____

_____

_____

_____

12. The wonderful message of the Christian faith is that we can be holy before God. Underline the ways that we become holy. Cross out those phrases that will not make us holy.

obedience to the Law	repentance for sins	believing in Jesus
giving money to the church	Jesus' righteousness	trust in Christ
purifying our hearts	trying hard to be good	studying
doing good works without faith	only acting like a Christian	God's grace

13. The apostle Paul tells us in Colossians 3:5–10, 12–14 that we are to put to death earthly things and to put on Christ. Fill in the chart.

compassionate hearts	sexual immorality	impurity	patience
covetousness	passion	evil desires	kindness
humility	meekness	anger	malice
slander	obscene talk	love	forgiveness
gentleness	lies	new self	gratitude

Things to Put to Death	Things to Put On as God's Chosen Ones

Getting Started 12.1

1. Write the words of your memory verse, Psalm 119:89–90. _____

_____

_____

_____

_____

   a. According to Psalm 119:89–90, how long will God's Word endure? _____

   b. How long will God continue to be faithful to his people? _____

2. Our world is not perfect. In spite of all the wonderful things about life, all people have problems. Underline the problems that you have experienced personally.

a friend moved away	a broken bone	a car accident
a parent's illness	loss of a grandparent	having something stolen
an argument with a friend	having surgery	a serious illness of your own
disappointment over a loss	guilt or shame for a sin	temptation to do something wrong

The Bible answers many of the questions people have about why there are problems in the world. Recall that sin brought a curse to the earth. Read the following passages in Genesis. Fill in the circle in front of the problem mentioned in the verse.

3. Genesis 3:16 (first half of the verse)
   ◯ pain in childbirth   ◯ thorns and thistles   ◯ hard-packed soil

4. Genesis 3:17 (last half of the verse)
   ◯ pollution and earthquakes   ◯ illnesses   ◯ curse on the ground

5. Genesis 3:18
   ◯ robberies and other thefts   ◯ broken homes   ◯ thorns and thistles

6. Genesis 3:19 (first half of the verse)
   ◯ hard work in farming   ◯ pain in childbirth   ◯ sicknesses

7. Genesis 3:19 (last half of the verse)
   ◯ death   ◯ natural disasters   ◯ thorns and thistles

8. Refer to the Biblical Truths in Lesson 4. Write either **harmony** or **disharmony with others**, **harmony** or **disharmony with God**, **harmony** or **disharmony with the earth**, or **harmony** or **disharmony within ourselves** below the appropriate pictures.

1. Complete the crossword puzzle. Use your student text to find the correct words.

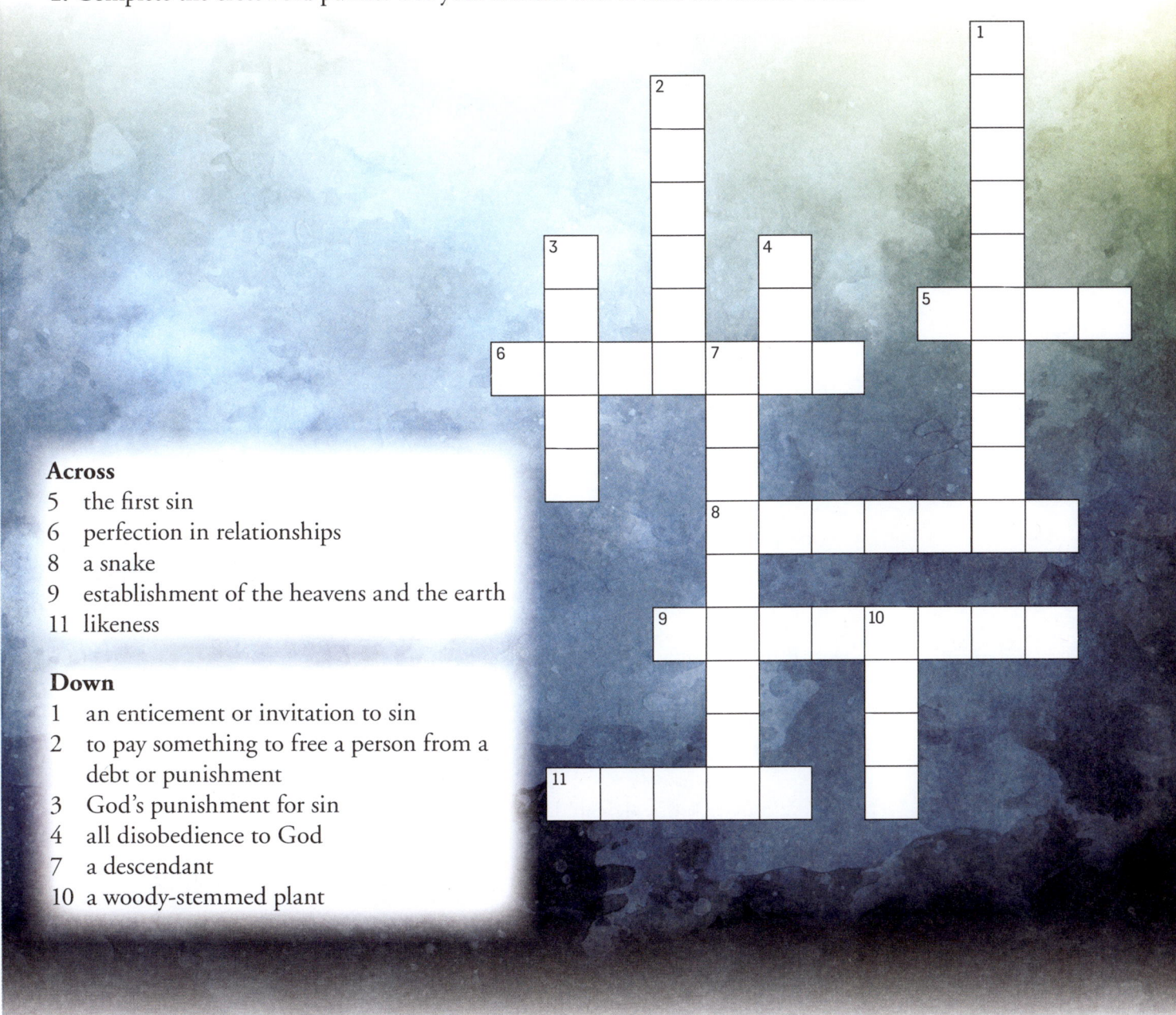

Across
5   the first sin
6   perfection in relationships
8   a snake
9   establishment of the heavens and the earth
11 likeness

Down
1   an enticement or invitation to sin
2   to pay something to free a person from a debt or punishment
3   God's punishment for sin
4   all disobedience to God
7   a descendant
10 a woody-stemmed plant

2. Complete the definition of redeem.

To _____ something in order to _____ a

person from a _____ or _____.

3. Underline all the examples of the concept of redemption.

A person paid the bail (a fine) for someone who has been unjustly charged with a crime.

A friend loaned another friend some money to pay for a meal.

Jesus, God the Son, died on the cross to pay the penalty we all deserve for our sins.

4. Read Romans 6:23. Answer the questions.

    a. What is the just punishment that we deserve for our sins? _____

    b. Who redeems us? _____

    c. How are we able to receive eternal life? _____

    _____

Write **creation**, **fall** or **redemption** to answer each worldview question.

5. _____ Where did I come from?

6. _____ Why are there so many problems in the world?

7. _____ Is there a God?

8. _____ Was the world ever without problems?

9. _____ What will happen to me after I die?

10. _____ What is my responsibility to the earth?

11. _____ Why am I able to think, choose, have
                                     feelings, and know right from wrong?

12. _____ Is there an answer for solving the world's problems?

13. _____ Will evil ever be defeated?

Does the paraphrased verse refer to the problem of sin or to God's solution for sin? Check the correct column.

	Problem	God's Solution
14. The reason the Son of God appeared was to destroy the works of the devil (1 John 3:8).		
15. All people have sinned and fall short of God's glory (Romans 3:23).		
16. Christ was delivered up for our trespasses and raised up to make us right with God (Romans 4:25).		
17. Just as sin came into the world through Adam, which brought death, so death spread to all people because all have sinned (Romans 5:12).		

Read the verses below the picture. Then decide which letter should go on the line. Letters may be used more than once.

A. God is just. Because of sin, he chose to end life on the earth through a great flood.

B. God established a covenant with his image-bearers.

C. Noah, who found favor with God, obeyed him.

D. Some people and animals were saved on the ark by God's grace.

| 1. Genesis 6:14–16 | 2. Genesis 9:8–17 | 3. Genesis 7:6–7, 24 |
| 4. Genesis 6:17–21 | 5. Genesis 7:8–9 | 6. Genesis 6:22 |

7. Read Hebrews 11:7. Answer the questions.

   a. How did Noah demonstrate faith in God's word? _____

   _____

   _____

   b. How did Noah show reverence for God? _____

   c. What did Noah become because of his faith in God? _____

   _____

   d. How do we become heirs of God's righteousness? _____

   _____

A covenant is a special promise or agreement. It can be unilateral, meaning just one of the two people or groups promises to do something. Or, it can be bilateral, meaning that both parties must do something; the covenant is conditional. Read each of the sentences below. Decide if the covenant described is unilateral or bilateral. Check the correct column.

	Unilateral Covenant	Bilateral Covenant
8. Adam and Eve would live forever in the garden of Eden as long as they did not eat from the Tree of the Knowledge of Good and Evil.		
9. God promised never to destroy the world again through a flood.		
10. God promises salvation, eternal life, for all who believe and trust in Jesus.		
11. God told Adam and Eve that he would send the Savior to strike Satan.		
12. God promises us new heavens and earth.		

Read the following Biblical Truths and explain how each truth relates to the story of Noah.

13. Biblical Truth 1: God is Truth and always tells us what is right and true.

_____

_____

14. Biblical Truth 4: God is the Creator.

_____

_____

15. Biblical Truth 7: Sin causes separation and disharmony between people and God.

_____

_____

16. Biblical Truth 18: God created his image-bearers to rule over his Earth.

_____

_____

17. Read 1 Peter 3:20–21. Answer the questions.

  a. How many people were brought safely through the floodwaters? _____

  b. What does Peter say the waters of the flood are like, or are pictures of? _____

1. Read Genesis 12:1–9 and answer the questions.
   a. What promise did God make to Abram in this passage?

   _____

   _____

   _____

   b. How did Abram know where to go? _____

   c. What was the land that God gave Abram known as?

   _____

   d. To whom did God promise to give the land after Abram?

   _____

2. Read Genesis 26:1–5. Answer the questions.

   a. What did God promise Isaac? _____

   _____

   b. Through whom would all the nations of the earth be

   blessed? _____

   _____

3. Through an unusual dream, God made a covenant with Jacob. The dream was of a ladder, extending from Earth to heaven. To complete the ladder puzzle, start with Jacob and go down. The last letter of Jacob is the first letter of the next word and its last letter is the first letter of the next word. Use the clues to help you write the words on the ladder.

   B. Through Abraham's family, the whole earth would be ___.

   C. The generations of offspring in a family are ___.

   D. The process of being saved through faith is ___.

   E. A group of people with its own land and government is

   a ___.

   F. The person who built the ark is ___.

   G. Jacob traveled from Beersheba to ___.

   H. Jacob had a dream when he went to sleep for the ___.

A. Jacob

B. _____

C. _____

D. _____

E. _____

F. _____

G. _____

H. _____

4. Write the events in the Word Bank into the time line.

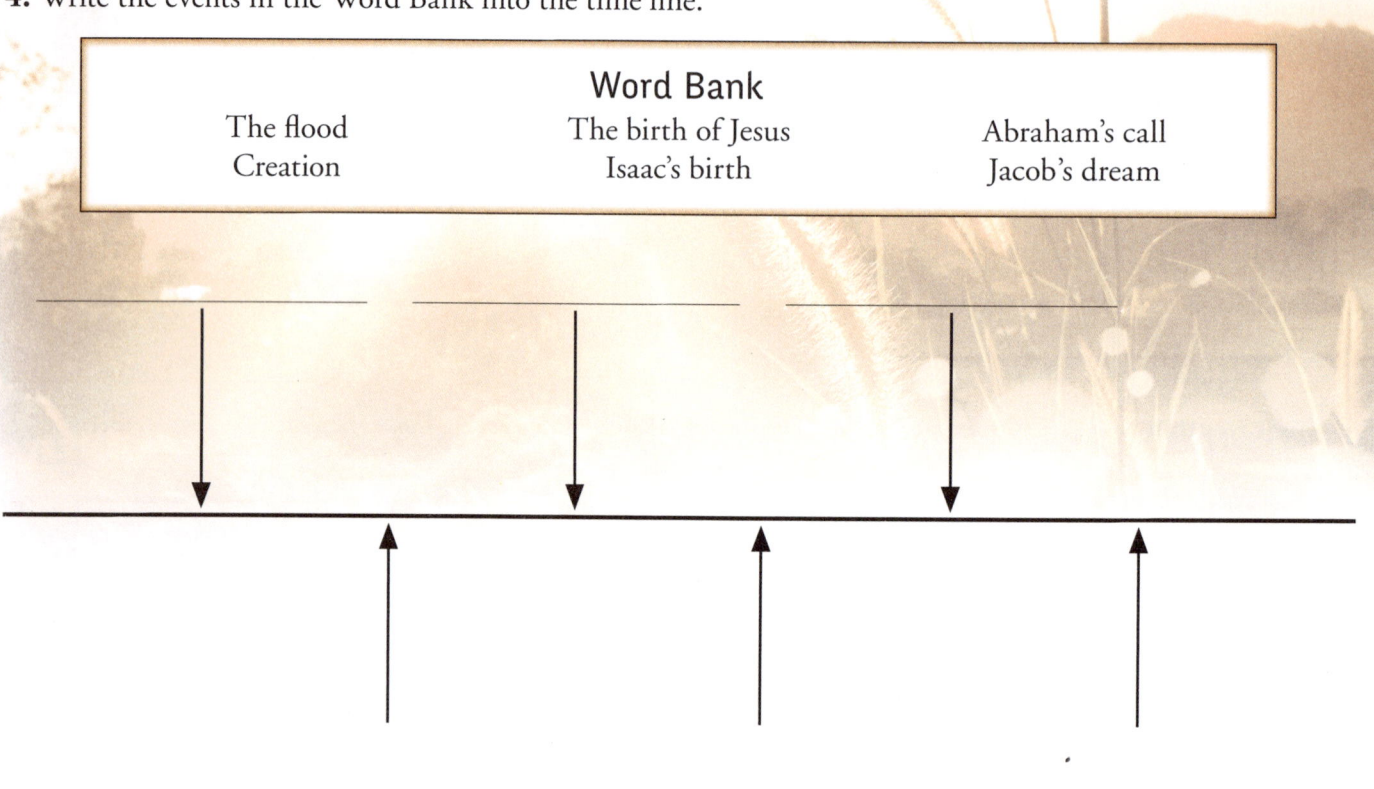

Word Bank

| The flood | The birth of Jesus | Abraham's call |
| Creation | Isaac's birth | Jacob's dream |

5. Underline all the things that were included in God's covenant with Jacob.

land	sheep	a church	God's protection
peace	stars	offspring	honor and respect
fame	good crops	nieces and nephews	a house

6. Read Galatians 3:29 and answer the questions.

a. How does God's promise to Abraham apply to you today? _____

_____

_____

b. What will you inherit as a child of God? _____

7. God made a covenant with three generations of one family. Write the names of those three people in order from first to last. _____

1. Read Psalm 119:89–90. How does this verse apply to the covenant made with Abraham, Isaac, and Jacob? _____

_____

Use the Word Bank to solve the riddles. Remember, not all the riddles will refer to people. Some of the words will not be used. Some words will be used twice.

Word Bank					
ark	Esau	Noah	Joseph	Abraham	rainbow
Isaac	Jacob	Jesus	David	Adam	Judah

2. _____ I am the sign of the covenant God made with Noah.

3. _____ I am the son who was favored over his brothers.

4. _____ I am the son who was chosen to be the heir of the covenant even before my birth.

5. _____ I am the obedient man who lived in the midst of evil people. I found favor in God's eyes.

6. _____ I am the son God promised to Abraham and Sarah despite their advanced ages.

7. _____ I am the promised Messiah, the offspring of Eve who crushed the work of Satan.

8. _____ I am the governor who forgave his brothers, knowing God can bring good even from sinful acts.

9. _____ I am the man who wrestled with God. God changed my name to Israel.

10. _____ I am the father of the Hebrew nation. God made a covenant with me and my heirs.

Joseph forgave his brothers. Read the verses related to forgiveness. Answer the questions.

11. In Matthew 6:14, what will God do when you forgive others?

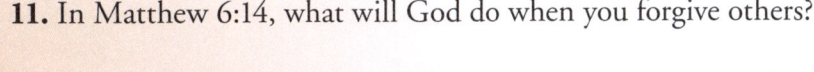

12. In Luke 17:3, what must you do for a brother who repents?

_____

13. In Ephesians 1:7, what do you have through the blood of Christ?

_____

14. In 1 John 1:9, what must you do to receive forgiveness for your sins?

_____

To play Biblical Truths Tic-Tac-Toe, read the statements below. Make an **X** in each box that has a Biblical Truth that relates to an event in the life of Joseph. Write the sentence number below the **X**.

Biblical Truth 10	Biblical Truth 12	Biblical Truth 15
Biblical Truth 20	Biblical Truth 1	Biblical Truth 17
Biblical Truth 13	Biblical Truth 3	Biblical Truth 16

15. God spoke the truth to Joseph through the dreams Joseph had as a youth.

16. Jacob and his sons raised sheep.

17. Joseph's brothers' jealousy and Jacob's sin of favoritism was destructive to the family.

18. The pharaoh appointed Joseph to store grain.

19. Joseph had a beautiful coat.

20. The book of Genesis tells the story of Joseph.

21. Joseph served Pharaoh, the country of Egypt, his brothers, and their children during the famine.

22. God made a covenant with Jacob.

23. Joseph was a Hebrew, one of God's chosen people.

24. The land of Canaan was blessed with good crops.

25. After Joseph died, his brothers preserved his bones.

Match the person to the description.

A. Joshua   B. Abraham   C. Moses   D. Isaac   E. Jacob

_____ **1.** He was the father of the special nation into which Jesus would be born.

_____ **2.** He had 12 sons.

_____ **3.** He was raised in a palace.

_____ **4.** He was the son of the father of the Hebrew nation.

_____ **5.** He was the Israelites' leader in Canaan.

Match the place to the event that took place there.

A. Egypt   B. Ur   C. Eden   D. Mount Sinai   E. Canaan

_____ **6.** God first announced his plan there.

_____ **7.** The Israelite people multiplied greatly there even though they were enslaved.

_____ **8.** God gave a promise to a man from there that he would be the father of a great nation.

_____ **9.** God first gave his laws in written form there.

_____ **10.** God's people got there after 40 years of wandering.

11. Write the words and reference for your memory verse. _____

_____

_____

12. With whom did God first make the covenant mentioned in the first part of your memory verse?

_____

13. Name a promise that God made to the Israelites.

_____

_____

_____

14. How is Jesus described in the second part of your memory verse?

_____

_____

_____

15. How should we respond to him in light of what this verse says?

_____

_____

Fill in the circle(s) to complete each sentence.

16. The Egyptians worried about the Israelites because . . .

◯ the Israelites controlled the pharaoh.   ◯ the Israelites brought plagues to their country.

◯ the Israelites multiplied so much they might take over Egypt.   ◯ the Israelites were Hebrews.

17. The Israelites did not always obey God because . . .

◯ he let them get lost on the way to Canaan.   ◯ he lived among them in the Holy Tent.

◯ they died.   ◯ they were sinners.   ◯ the pharaoh did not let them obey.

18. After Joshua died . . .

◯ Moses led the people.   ◯ the Israelites continued to follow God carefully.

◯ the Israelites conquered Canaan in seven years.   ◯ God sent judges to lead Israel.

19. The Israelites were finally a true nation when . . .

◯ they had people, land, and laws.   ◯ they got into wars with other nations.

◯ they chose their own rulers.   ◯ they worshipped idols.

20. God's plan to destroy the works of Satan . . .

◯ took place through the 10 plagues.   ◯ was fulfilled when the Israelites got to Canaan.

◯ would be fulfilled many years later through Abraham's descendant.

21. From Abraham, Isaac, Jacob, Moses, and Joshua, whom do you admire the most? Why?

_____

_____

_____

_____

_____

Mark each sentence **T** for true or **F** for false.

_____ **1.** The Hebrews were forced to become slaves in the land of Canaan.

_____ **2.** The king of Egypt grew afraid of the Hebrews, so he ordered their baby boys be killed.

_____ **3.** One Hebrew woman put her baby boy in a basket and hid it in the Jordan River.

_____ **4.** The king's daughter found the baby and named him *Moses*.

_____ **5.** When he was about 40 years old, Moses saw an Egyptian kill a Hebrew slave.

_____ **6.** Two Hebrew men witnessed the murder, so Moses ran away to the country of Midian.

_____ **7.** God spoke to Moses from a bush that was on fire but did not burn up.

_____ **8.** God told Moses to take off his sandals because the place where he stood was holy.

_____ **9.** God said he had seen Moses' suffering and would restore him to leadership in Egypt.

_____ **10.** God said he was the God of Abraham, Isaac, and Jacob.

11. Rewrite the false sentences so that they are true.

_____

_____

_____

_____

Write the letters to match the Bible verses with the correct titles. Two verses match each title.

12. The Hebrew Slaves: _____ , _____

13. The Birth of Moses: _____ , _____

14. Moses Kills an Egyptian: _____ , _____

15. God Calls Moses: _____ , _____

A. Acts 7:17
B. Exodus 2:11–12
C. Exodus 3:10
D. Exodus 2:10
E. Hebrews 11:23
F. Exodus 2:15
G. Exodus 1:22
H. Acts 7:31–32

16. What order did the pharaoh give concerning the Hebrew babies? Why was it evil? _____

_____

_____

17. What did Moses' sister do for him? _____

_____

_____

_____

_____

18. When Moses saw an Egyptian beating a Hebrew, he killed the Egyptian. How should you react when you see someone mistreating someone else? _____

_____

_____

19. Read Psalm 103:6–12. Despite Moses' past sin, God called him to lead the Hebrew people. Why? _____

_____

_____

20. Read the story. Answer the question.

Caleb was mean to his sister at breakfast. When he got to school, he got into a fight with his best friend. He was rude when a teacher called on him. He shoved a teammate at practice. Now Caleb feels terrible and just wants to be alone. He does not think that even God would want anything to do with him.

What would you tell Caleb? _____

_____

_____

_____

Match the Bible verses with the correct titles. Two verses match each title.

A. Exodus 11:5   B. Exodus 14:13–14   C. Exodus 12:29   D. Exodus 14:22

1. The Plagues of Egypt: ____, ____   **2.** The Exodus: ____, ____

What happened when Moses and Aaron asked for the Israelites' freedom? Circle the answers.

3. What was the king's response?   He said yes.   He said no.   He threatened them with jail.

4. What was God's response?   He sent the king a dream.   He sent a plague.   He sent an army.

5. How many times did Moses and Aaron approach the king?   12   7   2   10

6. Number and identify each plague in the order God sent it to the Egyptians.

7. What finally made the king of Egypt change his mind? _____

_____

8. What did the Israelites have to do to protect their families from the last plague? _____

_____

_____

9. What Jewish feast today commemorates that event? _____

10. Why is Jesus called the Passover Lamb? _____

_____

Mark your answer to each question by filling in the circle(s).

11. About how many Israelites left Egypt for the Promised Land?

○ 10,000 ○ 10,000,000 ○ 1,000,000 ○ 100,000

12. What did the Egyptians give the Israelites for their journey?

○ gold ○ cows ○ clothing ○ silver

13. Where did the Israelites first camp on their journey?

○ beside the Nile River ○ beside the Red Sea ○ beside Canaan

14. What is another name for the journey that the Israelites began?

○ exodus ○ exile ○ caravan ○ convoy

15. What did the Lord tell Moses to do so the Israelites could escape the Egyptians?

○ cry out to the Lord ○ stretch his hand over the sea ○ ask the king for mercy
○ sacrifice a lamb ○ harden his heart ○ lift up his staff ○ stand in the water

16. How did the Red Sea part so that the Israelites were able to cross it to escape?

○ An earthquake split the water. ○ A wind blew all night to divide the waters.

17. What happened to the pharaoh and the Egyptian soldiers who were chasing the Israelites?

○ The Lord hardened their hearts. ○ They drowned. ○ They gave up and went home.
○ They tried to cross the sea. ○ They repented. ○ Their chariots stuck in the mud.
○ The water covered them up. ○ They panicked. ○ They cried out to the Lord.

18. Read Exodus 15:1–2. What did Moses and the people do after the miracle?

_____

_____

19. Read Exodus 15:20–21. What did Moses' sister do after the miracle?

_____

_____

_____

20. How should you respond when you see God work a miracle in your own life?

_____

_____

1. A commandment is an order to do or not do something. Complete the table below. If a commandment is positive, rewrite it in negative form; if it is negative, rewrite it in positive form. Rephrase the commandment. The first two are done for you.

	Do this (+)	**Do not do this (-)**
A.	**Make sure that I am first and most important in your life.**	You must not have any other god before me.
B.	**Worship only me.**	You must not make idols.
C.		You must not misuse the name of the Lord your God.
D.	Remember the Sabbath day, by keeping it holy.	
E.	Honor your father and mother.	
F.		You must not murder.
G.		You must not commit adultery.
H.		You must not steal.
I.		You must not testify falsely against your neighbor.
J.		You must not covet.

2. What are the Ten Commandments? _____

3. Read 1 John 5:3 and 2 John 1:6. What do these verses say about God's commandments?

_____

_____

4. How is Peter's description of the church in 1 Peter 2:9 like the promise God gave to the Israelites in Exodus 19:4–6? _____

_____

5. What was the purpose of the tabernacle? _____

_____

6. Find all the terms related to the tabernacle.

```
K L A M P S T A N D G L O R Y
B M B S N O M R Q O X X U O D
I N C E N S E C W T H D Y L R
S E C I F I R C A S W Q P W U
S R P H U R P R I E S T S M Y
A V E T P B Z B L D H H T F M
D Y F T O P J L S O H R E H B
L S I B A B D U O L C O N O M
S B C Y J W J D E D Z N T L B
S R K C O V E N A N T E S Y R
C O U R T Y A R D B Q M E W E
O P H E J R A T L A F R H P A
W E I L P D C W R U I W C O D
J M F F W A U K V F W O O D I
K R Y Y U D B D B R O N Z E K
```

altar	glory
ark	holy
bread	incense
bronze	lampstand
chest	priests
cloud	sacrifices
courtyard	tent
covenant	throne
dwell	water
fire	wood

Match the Bible verses with the correct titles. Two verses match each title.

A. Exodus 25:1–2, 8   B. Exodus 20:3

C. Exodus 40:34   D. Exodus 20:8

7. The Ten Commandments: ____ , ____

8. The Tabernacle: ____ , ____

9. What did the Lord's presence look like on the tabernacle by day? _____

10. What did it look like at night? _____

11. How might these miraculous sights have made you feel if you had traveled with the Israelites?

_____

_____

1. Number the pictures in the order that they happened.

Moses tells the people to obey
Joshua, their new leader.

At night, the Israelites are led
by the pillar of fire.

Moses tells the 12 men to go
into Canaan.

Moses looks at God's promised
land that he may not enter.

Moses and Aaron ask God
to provide water.

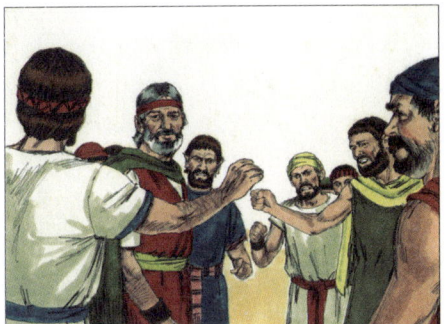

The Israelites argue they
should all return to Egypt.

Match the character with the action to complete the sentence.

_____ **2.** Joshua

_____ **3.** Moses

_____ **4.** Aaron

_____ **5.** Caleb

_____ **6.** The first generation

_____ **7.** Ten men

_____ **8.** The Lord

_____ **9.** The second generation

_____ **10.** Abraham

A. also grumbled and complained about life in the desert.

B. was the first person to receive God's promise about Canaan.

C. felt like grasshoppers.

D. died before his brother did.

E. all died before setting foot in the Promised Land.

F. encouraged the Israelites to follow the Law of Moses.

G. climbed Mount Nebo.

H. gave a good report, with Joshua, after spying in Canaan.

I. kept his promise to make Israel a nation with its own land.

Read the sentences. Underline the word or phrase that best completes the sentence.

11. When the Israelites were close to Canaan, God told Moses to send a leader from each tribe to (negotiate a treaty with its people / tell the Canaanites to worship God / to explore the land).

12. The twelve reported that the land of Canaan (was worse than Egypt / flowed with milk and honey).

13. They said the people of Canaan (were stronger than the Israelites / were easy to conquer).

14. After hearing the men's report, the Israelites were (confused / afraid / thankful for God's leading).

15. God decided to punish the first generation of Israelites for their grumbling and lack of faith in him by (turning them into pillars of salt / forbidding them from entering Canaan / sending snakes to bite them).

Answer the questions.

16. When the second generation of Israelites complained about not having enough food and water, what did God tell Moses to do? _____
_____

17. How did Moses disobey God? _____

18. How did God punish Moses for his disobedience? _____

19. What did God allow Moses to do before he died? _____

20. Who led the Israelites after Moses? _____

Read Joshua 1:6–11. Circle the answer(s).

21. What did God tell Joshua and the Israelites to be as they entered the land of Canaan?
    brave   quiet   strong   sneaky   courageous   proud   hardworking

22. What else did God tell Joshua and the Israelites they must always be careful to do?
    pack their provisions   meditate on the Law   listen to Aaron   surrender to their enemies

23. What did God promise the Israelites would receive if they were careful to do this?
    strength   land   livestock   success   prosperity   courage   children

24. How can you be strong and courageous in your daily life? _____
_____

25. What are some things you can do to help you meditate on and obey God's laws?
_____
_____

Mark the statements **T** for true or **F** for false.

_____ **1.** After the Hebrews conquered Canaan, they served God while Joshua was alive.

_____ **2.** When Joshua died, they began to worship Moses.

_____ **3.** As punishment, God sent Israel's enemies to attack and defeat his people.

_____ **4.** When the Israelites repented and cried to God for help, he sent strong leaders to help them.

_____ **5.** These strong leaders were called *kings*.

_____ **6.** After these leaders helped Israel defeat their enemies, the people turned back to worship God.

_____ **7.** After a few years of peace, the Israelites would disobey God again.

_____ **8.** The Israelites repeated the sin cycle for more than 3,000 years.

9. Rewrite the false sentences so that they are true.

_____

_____

_____

_____

10. Label the stages of the cycle of sin.

A. _____   B. _____

E. _____   C. _____

D. _____

11. Use the letters from the diagram above to match the Bible verses to the stages of the sin cycle.

_____ Judges 20:26   _____ Judges 10:6   _____ Judges 3:15

_____ Judges 2:14   _____ Joshua 22:4

Fill in the circle(s) to mark your answers.

12. How old was Joshua when he died?

◯ 80 years old   ◯ 30 years old   ◯ 110 years old   ◯ 96 years old

13. Who led Israel right after Joshua died?

◯ Samson   ◯ the leaders who outlived Joshua   ◯ Deborah   ◯ Gideon

14. What idols did Israel serve?

◯ Baal   ◯ Ashtoreth   ◯ Ephraim   ◯ the gods of the people around them

15. How many times did Israel walk through the cycle of sin?

◯ 300 times   ◯ 5 times   ◯ 12 times   ◯ too many times

16. Some of the most famous judges were Deborah, Gideon, and Samson. Read the Bible verses. Match them to the appropriate picture.

A. Judges 4:4–5   B. Judges 16:10   C. Judges 6:38

_____   _____   _____

Unscramble the words. Write one or two sentences about each word to explain how it relates to this lesson on the history of Israel.

17. COVANNTE: _____

_____

18. OBEDDISIECNE: _____

_____

19. EMESNIE: _____

_____

20. TIPY: _____

_____

21. EPACE: _____

_____

1. Write the words and reference for your memory verse. _____

_____

_____

2. A reporter from *The Jerusalem Post* is writing a story about King Saul. Since you (Samuel) know Saul well, you are able to provide the information the reporter needs for the story. Write the missing words on the blank lines. Refer to Topic 1 in your Student Textbook for help.

Reporter: I understand that you are the prophet who anointed Saul as the first king of Israel. Did you have some reservations about Israel's having a king?

Samuel: Yes. The (a) _____ of Israel came to my home in (b) _____. They said that my sons are greedy for money, so they accepted (c) _____ and perverted justice.

Reporter: When the elders of Israel told you that they wanted a king, didn't you feel rejected?

Samuel: God told me that the people were not (d) _____ me. Actually, they were (e) _____ him as their (f) _____. Then God told me everything a king would do to Israel's people. He said that a king would take their (g) _____ and assign them to his (h) _____ and charioteers. He would make some generals and captains in his army. Others would be forced to (i) _____ his fields and harvest his crops.

Reporter: That sounds harsh, but a king won't take our daughters, will he?

Samuel: On the contrary. Some of the Israel's daughters will be forced to cook and (j) _____. Others will have to make (k) _____ for the king. People will have to give up their best (l) _____ and vineyards. The king will take a tenth of their (m) _____ and grape harvest. He'll even take a tenth of all domestic animals. Israel will beg for (n) _____.

Reporter: Do you think the elders will change their minds and accept God as their king?

Samuel: Unfortunately, they won't change their minds. Now I pray God chooses the right man for the job.

Saul disobeyed the Lord's command to destroy the Amalekites completely. When he spared their king and many of their animals, he demonstrated incomplete obedience to God. Read the scenarios below. Write **complete** if the student shows complete obedience and **incomplete** if he or she does not.

3. _____ Mom told Evan to take out the trash. Evan got his brother to do it.

4. _____ Mrs. Marx assigned 25 math problems. Ben only did 15 of them.

5. _____ Dad asked Jackson to clean his room. Jackson cleaned it.

6. _____ Anna was supposed to be home by 5 pm. She came home at 6.

7. _____ Mr. Smith told the class to work quietly. Zach kept talking.

8. _____ Charley answered all the assigned science questions.

9. _____ Matthew listened to his coach and followed his instructions.

10. Read the verses about obedience. Write the blessing that comes as a result of obedience.

Scripture	Blessing
Deuteronomy 4:1	
Deuteronomy 6:2	
Joshua 1:7	
Psalm 119:1–2	

11. Read Matthew 21:28–32. Answer the questions.

   a. What command did the father give his two sons? _____

   _____

   b. What did the older boy say? _____

   _____

   c. Later on, he changed his mind. What did he do then?

   _____

   d. What did the younger boy say? _____

   e. What did he do? _____

   f. Which boy obeyed his father? _____

   g. If you say that you will obey, but you don't follow through, what are you really doing?

_____

Remember that God told Samuel not to judge Jesse's sons by their appearance or height. The Lord doesn't see things the way you see them. People judge by outward appearance, but the Lord looks at the heart. Read each sentence. Write **yes** next to the ones that show a godly attitude.

1. Marcos helps his church by working in the nursery without pay. _____

2. Laurie helps her disabled brother when her mom tells her to, but she resents it. _____

3. DeShon coaches the new players on his football team without being asked. _____

4. Natalie visits the elderly in a nearby rest home as a volunteer. _____

5. Dixon gladly gives a portion of his allowance to the Lord. _____

6. Grant sings in his church's praise team only so people will like him. _____

David took only five stones with him when he went to kill the giant, Goliath. Each stone could represent one of David's character traits. Read the sentences and the verses. Write the letter of the verse that best matches the character trait described.

7. ____ David showed initiative in volunteering to fight Goliath.

8. ____ David trusted God.

9. ____ David demonstrated loyalty to his country by defeating one of its Philistine enemies.

10. ____ David had confidence that God would help him.

11. ____ David showed his reverence for God by addressing Goliath's insults.

A. Psalm 31:14

B. Ecclesiastes 9:10

C. Proverbs 18:24

D. Philippians 4:13

E. Deuteronomy 13:4

12. The Israelites thought Goliath was too big to fight; David thought he was too big to miss! Tell about a time when you took on a challenge that was hard for you. How did your faith in God help you defeat your "giant"?

_____

_____

_____

_____

_____

13. Saul was envious of David. Read the verses about envy and answer the questions.

    a. Proverbs 14:30. What does envy do to a person physically? _____

    _____

    b. Proverbs 23:17. Instead of envying sinners, what should a Christian's response be?

    _____

    _____

Mark your answer to each question by filling in the appropriate circle(s).

14. How many sons did Jesse have?

    ○ 7   ○ 10   ○ 8   ○ 2

15. Of Jesse's sons, which was David?

    ○ the oldest   ○ the middle   ○ the fourth   ○ the youngest

16. What did Samuel do to show that God had selected David as king?

    ○ anointed him   ○ crowned him   ○ blessed him

17. What instrument did David play for Saul?

    ○ guitar   ○ harp   ○ flute   ○ trumpet

18. How did David's musical talent help Saul?

    ○ by calming him   ○ by entertaining him   ○ by putting him to sleep   ○ by defeating his enemies

19. Why did Saul feel threatened by David?

    ○ because David had brothers   ○ because the people loved David   ○ because Saul was ill
    ○ because David was brave   ○ because David was young   ○ because David was handsome

20. Why did Saul attempt to kill David?

    ○ because David was evil   ○ because David insulted him   ○ because Saul was jealous
    ○ because David was disloyal   ○ because David hated Saul   ○ because David loved God

21. Saul was so jealous of David that he succumbed to the temptation to attempt murder. Tell about a time in your life when you were jealous, but overcame the temptation to sin.

    _____

    _____

    _____

Write **David**, **Saul**, or **Samuel** to answer each riddle.

1. I anointed two kings in obedience to God's command. _____

2. I warned the people of Israel against having any king but God. _____

3. I took care of my father Jesse's sheep. _____

4. I was the first king of Israel. _____

5. I played my harp for the king. _____

6. I was the last judge of Israel. _____

7. I fought and killed an enemy soldier no one else was willing to fight. _____

8. I disobeyed God by not killing King Agag of the Amalekites nor the sheep or cattle. _____

9. I was praised by the people of Israel for killing tens of thousands. Saul was jealous of me. _____

10. I disobeyed God by offering a sacrifice only priests were allowed to offer. _____

11. My sons and I were killed in battle because I was disobedient to God. _____

12. Saul consulted a medium—a witch or a sorcerer. Because of this evil practice, God declared that he and his sons would die in battle. Read what God's Word has to say about the practice of witchcraft. Answer the questions.

a. Leviticus 19:26. Should anyone practice fortune-telling or

witchcraft? _____

b. 2 Chronicles 33:6. What evil practices did King Manasseh

engage in? _____

_____

c. How did God feel about King Manasseh's evil? _____

d. Micah 5:12. What does God say he will do to sorcerers, witches, or fortune-tellers?

_____

_____

e. Revelation 21:8. Should Christians avoid occult practices? Why? _____

_____

_____

13. After Saul died, David became king. God promised that a descendant of David, the second king of Israel, would rule forever. Unscramble the words related to God's promise. Then unscramble the circled letters and write the promised King's title.

MYAR ⬜⬜⬜⬜

RAOVIS ⬜⬜⬜⬜⬜⬜

HEEMETLHB ⬜⬜⬜⬜⬜⬜⬜⬜⬜

LIEBARG ⬜⬜⬜⬜⬜⬜⬜

DAVDI ⬜⬜⬜⬜⬜

SEENANDDCT ⬜⬜⬜⬜⬜⬜⬜⬜⬜⬜

⬜⬜⬜⬜⬜⬜⬜

Study the genealogy chart. Answer the questions. Remember that the numbers stand for generations of Abraham's family.

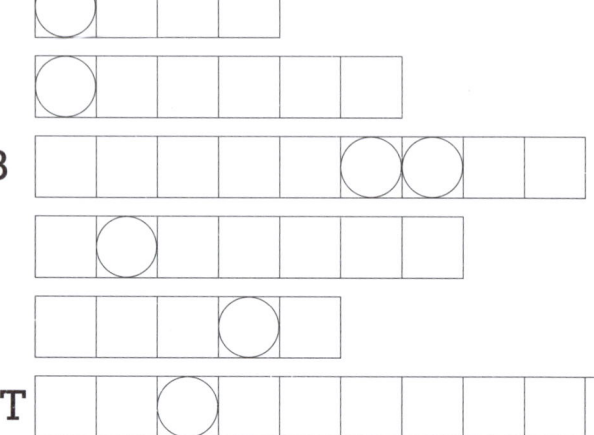

14. How many generations are there between Judah and David? _____

15. Who received God's promised agreement or covenant?

_____

_____

_____

_____

Numbers stand for generations.

16. How many generations are there between David and Jesus? _____

17. Who is the King who fulfills God's covenant with David? _____

18. David prepared his son Solomon to rule in his place. How do your parents prepare you to serve God? Write two sentences. _____

_____

Mark your answer to each question by filling in the appropriate circle(s).

1. What buildings did Solomon complete after 20 years of construction?
- ○ the synagogue of David
- ○ the temple
- ○ the tabernacle
- ○ Solomon's palace

2. What gift did Solomon ask of the Lord?
- ○ popularity
- ○ wisdom
- ○ fame
- ○ love
- ○ many wives
- ○ riches
- ○ good looks

3. How did Solomon disobey the Lord?
- ○ by building the temple
- ○ by marrying foreign women
- ○ by worshipping the gods of his wives

4. What could Solomon speak about with authority?
- ○ plant life
- ○ medicine
- ○ folklore
- ○ politics
- ○ animal life
- ○ comets

5. What tribe would Solomon's son inherit as king?
- ○ Asher
- ○ Gad
- ○ Ephraim
- ○ Dan
- ○ Judah
- ○ Manasseh

6. Solomon was both wise and materialistic. Read the verses and answer the questions.

a. 1 Kings 4:21. Who paid taxes (tribute) to Solomon and continued to serve him? _____

_____

b. 1 Kings 4:26. How many horses did Solomon own? _____

c. 1 Kings 4:32. How many proverbs and psalms did he write? _____

d. 1 Kings 4:33. On what could Solomon speak with authority? _____

_____

Underline the word(s) that best complete each sentence.

7. King Solomon built the temple on (Mount Moriah, Mount Nebo), which was the site that King David had selected.

8. The temple was beautifully decorated with carvings of (ancient kings, cherubim).

9. Solomon furnished the temple with (lampstands, basins, and tables; couches, drapes, and windows) similar to the way the tabernacle was furnished.

10. Reread Samuel's warning to Israel in 1 Samuel 8:10–17. Did Samuel's words come true? Why?

_____

_____

11. Read about the visit of the Queen of Sheba to Solomon's court in 1 Kings 10:1–13. Summarize her visit in your own words.

_____

_____

_____

_____

12. Toward the end of Solomon's life, he became dissatisfied with his great wisdom. Read Solomon's words in Ecclesiastes 1:1–18. Answer the questions.

   a. What do you think Solomon means when he says that everything is meaningless? Do you agree that there is no meaning in life? Why or why not? _____

   _____

   b. Do you agree with Solomon's assessment that there is nothing new under the sun? Why or why not?

   _____

   c. In verse 11, Solomon says that no one remembers former generations. Is this true? Why or why not?

   _____

   d. In verses 16 and 17, Solomon says that pursuing knowledge is like chasing the wind. Why do you think Solomon became bored or dissatisfied with seeking knowledge?

   _____

   e. In verse 18, Solomon says that wisdom produces sorrow or sadness. Do you think Solomon would have been as unhappy if he had stayed close to God throughout his life? Why or why not?

   _____

Match the way Solomon disobeyed God with the Bible verse.

13. _____ Solomon worshipped the goddess Ashtoreth.

14. _____ Solomon built a shrine to the idol Chemosh.

15. _____ Solomon built shrines for all his foreign wives.

16. _____ Solomon had 700 wives of royal birth and 300 concubines.

A. 1 Kings 11:7
B. 1 Kings 11:5
C. 1 Kings 11:8
D. 1 Kings 11:3

Name ______________________ Date ______________

Getting Started and Topic 1 15.1

Match the person or people to the descriptions.

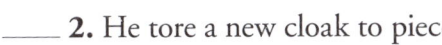

A. Solomon B. Rehoboam C. Jeroboam D. Ahijah E. Shemaiah
F. the older counselors G. the young advisers H. Israel I. Judah

____ **1.** He was put in charge of the workers from the tribes of Ephraim and Manasseh.

____ **2.** He tore a new cloak to pieces.

____ **3.** Its people wanted to do less work and pay less in taxes.

____ **4.** He tried to kill his servant.

____ **5.** They gave advice to increase the people's burden.

____ **6.** He refused to listen to the people.

____ **7.** Their advice was rejected.

____ **8.** He told the king not to fight against his relatives.

____ **9.** King David was from this tribe who remained loyal to his family.

10. Answer the questions to explain what the tearing of the coat meant.

a. Who met Jeroboam outside Jerusalem? ______________

b. Into how many pieces was the cloak torn? ______________

c. What happened to 10 pieces of the cloak? ______________

____

d. What did the pieces symbolize? ______________

____

____

e. Whose sin led to this event? ______________

f. What was his sin? ______________

g. What was his son's name? ______________

h. To what tribe did that king and his son belong? ______________

11. What is a prophet? ______________

12. Read Leviticus 19:32 and 1 Peter 5:5. Do these verses describe how Rehoboam treated the elders who served his father, King Solomon? Why or why not? ______________

____

____

13. Read Proverbs 28:16. Does this verse suggest that Rehoboam made a wise decision? Why or why not?

_____

_____

14. Whose advice should Rehoboam have followed? Circle the answer.

his friends'   the older men's   Solomon's   Ahijah's

15. Read 1 Kings 12:13–14 and Matthew 11:28–30. Which king would you rather follow? Why? _____

_____

_____

_____

_____

16. What was the result of Rehoboam's response to the people?

_____

_____

_____

17. Who stopped Rehoboam and the men of Judah and Benjamin from going to war? How?

_____

_____

18. Underline the correct location.

Jeroboam fled to (Egypt, Israel, Jerusalem, Judah, Shechem).

The City of David is called (Egypt, Israel, Jerusalem, Judah, Shechem).

Solomon was buried in (Egypt, Israel, Jerusalem, Judah, Shechem).

Jeroboam ruled (Egypt, Israel, Jerusalem, Judah, Shechem).

He made (Egypt, Israel, Jerusalem, Judah, Shechem) the new capital.

Rehoboam ruled (Egypt, Israel, Jerusalem, Judah, Shechem).

Rehoboam lived in the city of (Egypt, Israel, Jerusalem, Judah, Shechem).

19. Write the words and reference for your memory verse. _____

_____

_____

Match the verses to each picture.

A. Amos 5:12   B. Amos 3:8   C. Amos 3:11   D. Amos 5:11   E. Amos 1:1   F. Amos 3:6

1. _____

2. _____

3. _____

4. _____

5. _____

6. _____

7. Compare Psalm 106:19–21 and Hosea 8:5–6. What is similar?

_____

_____

What is different? _____

_____

8. Why was it wrong for the Israelites to worship the calf?

_____

_____

_____

_____

9. What should the Israelites have done instead? _____

Mark each sentence **T** for true or **F** for false.

_____ **10.** Though Amos was from Judah, he spoke against Israel.

_____ **11.** Amos said the Israelites loved and honored truth-tellers.

_____ **12.** The poor trampled on the rich and took their grain.

_____ **13.** The Israelites worshipped idols at the shrines of the king.

_____ **14.** God promised the Israelites he would exile Amos to a foreign land beyond Damascus.

_____ **15.** Hosea's name means _salvation_.

_____ **16.** Hosea said the Israelites had no faithfulness, no kindness, and no knowledge of God.

_____ **17.** The Israelites made idols with their gold and silver.

_____ **18.** The Israelites planted wind and would harvest a whirlwind.

_____ **19.** God promised Assyria would be forced to serve the Israelites.

20. Rewrite the false sentences so that they are true.

_____

_____

_____

_____

_____

21. Read Galatians 6:8. List one way to please the Spirit in each of the following:

a. At home: _____

_____

b. At school: _____

_____

c. At church: _____

_____

d. In your community: _____

_____

Mark your answer to each question by filling in the circle(s).

1. What kingdom did God use to punish the northern kingdom of Israel?

○ Babylon   ○ Egypt   ○ Assyria

○ Judah   ○ Iraq   ○ Lebanon

2. Who was king of the nation God used to punish the northern kingdom of Israel?

○ Belshazzar   ○ Hoshea   ○ Shalmaneser

○ Cyrus   ○ Nebuchadnezzar

3. Who was the king of Israel when God finally punished the nation?

○ Rehoboam   ○ Solomon   ○ Hosea   ○ Hoshea   ○ David

4. What country did Israel ask to help them shake free from the power of the Assyrians?

○ Egypt   ○ Babylon   ○ Ephraim   ○ Lebanon   ○ Iraq

5. What did the king of Assyria do to the king of Israel when he heard of the plan with Egypt?

○ praised him   ○ rewarded him   ○ put him in prison   ○ demanded tribute

○ seized him   ○ released him   ○ gave him more responsibility

6. How many years did Assyria besiege Samaria?

○ nine   ○ seven   ○ three   ○ two   ○ twelve

7. Instead of worshipping God, whose worship did the Israelites copy?

○ the Egyptians'   ○ the Medes'   ○ that of pagan nations the Lord had driven out

8. Whom did God send to the Israelites to warn them of their sins?

○ Elijah and Elisha   ○ Amos and Hosea   ○ Ezra and Nehemiah

9. How did the people of the northern kingdom of Israel respond to the prophets' messages?

_____

10. Why did God send the people of the northern kingdom of Israel into captivity in Assyria?

_____

_____

_____

11. Pretend you are a citizen of the northern kingdom of Israel. The Assyrians are attacking your city, Samaria. While you still have time, write a letter to a friend who lives in the southern kingdom of Judah. Explain why the Assyrians are attacking your city, what you expect will happen if they win, and how the people of the kingdom of Judah can keep from being punished by God like the kingdom of Israel is now being punished.

Dear _____,

_____

_____

_____

_____

_____

_____

_____

_____

_____

Your friend,

_____

12. Read Ezekiel 20:39–41. Answer the questions.

a. What will God require from Israel when its people abandon their idols and worship him?

_____

b. What will the nations see as a result? _____

13. Read Psalm 76:11. What gifts or tribute can you give to God? _____

_____

_____

_____

1. How long did the southern kingdom of Judah exist? _____

2. How many kings and queens ruled the southern kingdom of Judah? _____

3. What two prophets spoke God's messages of warning and promise to the people of Judah?

_____

4. Write a checkmark in the column with the name of the prophet to whom the sentence refers.

		Isaiah	Jeremiah
A.	He saw a vision of Judah and Jerusalem during the reign of four of Judah's kings.		
B.	God spoke to him during the first year Nebuchadnezzar was king of Babylon.		
C.	He told of God's promise to send a Son who would rule forever as the Prince of Peace.		
D.	He told the people of Judah that God had reared them and brought them up like a father does his children.		
E.	He told the people of Judah that God was going to remove all the sounds of joy and gladness from the nation because of their sins.		
F.	He told the people of Judah that God would no longer listen to their prayers because of their sins.		
G.	He told the people of Judah that one day God would raise up a King named *The Lord Is Our Righteousness*.		
H.	He told the people of Judah that their whole country would become a wasteland because of their sins.		
I.	He told the people of Judah that one day they would no longer walk in darkness of sin, but would see the light.		
J.	He told the people of Judah that they would serve the king of Babylon for 70 years.		

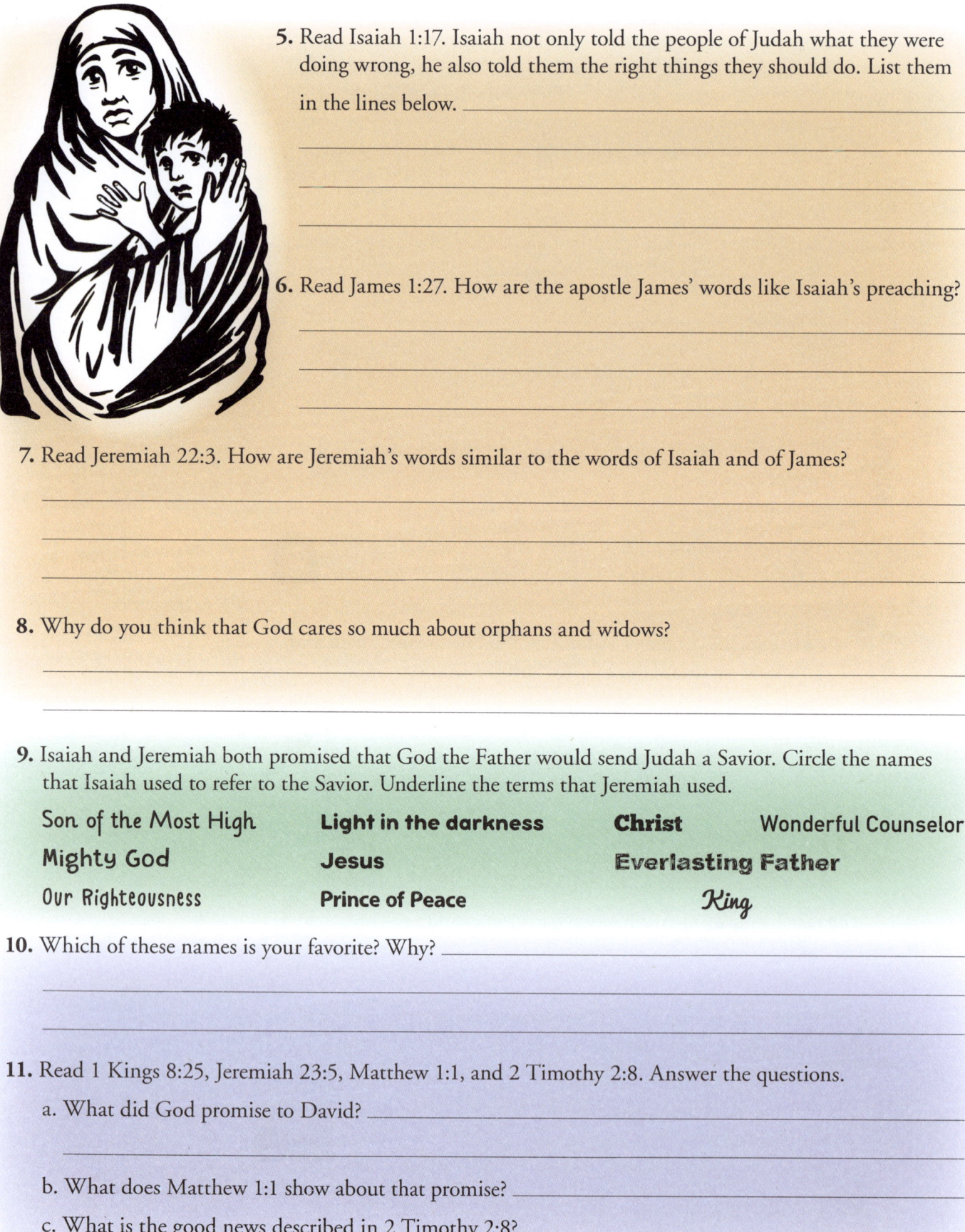

5. Read Isaiah 1:17. Isaiah not only told the people of Judah what they were doing wrong, he also told them the right things they should do. List them in the lines below. _____

_____

_____

_____

6. Read James 1:27. How are the apostle James' words like Isaiah's preaching?

_____

_____

_____

7. Read Jeremiah 22:3. How are Jeremiah's words similar to the words of Isaiah and of James?

_____

_____

_____

8. Why do you think that God cares so much about orphans and widows?

_____

_____

9. Isaiah and Jeremiah both promised that God the Father would send Judah a Savior. Circle the names that Isaiah used to refer to the Savior. Underline the terms that Jeremiah used.

Son of the Most High	**Light in the darkness**	**Christ** Wonderful Counselor
Mighty God	**Jesus**	**Everlasting Father**
Our Righteousness	**Prince of Peace**	*King*

10. Which of these names is your favorite? Why? _____

_____

_____

11. Read 1 Kings 8:25, Jeremiah 23:5, Matthew 1:1, and 2 Timothy 2:8. Answer the questions.

a. What did God promise to David? _____

_____

b. What does Matthew 1:1 show about that promise? _____

c. What is the good news described in 2 Timothy 2:8? _____

_____

1. Number the pictures in the order that they happened.

Zedekiah is captured.
_____

The temple is set on fire.
_____

Zedekiah's sons are killed.
_____

The people are taken captive.
_____

Zedekiah escapes Jerusalem.
_____

The people of Jerusalem starve.
_____

Fill in the circle(s) to answer each question.

2. Which king rebelled against Babylon?   ◯ King Nebuchadnezzar   ◯ King Zedekiah

3. Which king marched against Jerusalem?   ◯ King Nebuchadnezzar   ◯ King Zedekiah

4. What did the people experience due to the siege of their city?   ◯ plague   ◯ famine

5. What did King Zedekiah and his army do when the Babylonians broke through the walls of Jerusalem?
◯ surrendered   ◯ fought as hard as they could   ◯ escaped   ◯ negotiated a treaty

6. What did the Babylonians do to Zedekiah's sons? ◯ blinded them ◯ enslaved them ◯ killed them

7. What did the Babylonians do to the king of Judah when they captured him?
◯ put him in prison ◯ killed him ◯ blinded him ◯ offered him to their gods as a sacrifice

8. Where were the king of Judah's soldiers then?   ◯ back in Jerusalem   ◯ in the enemy camp

9. What did the Babylonians set on fire?   ◯ everything   ◯ the temple   ◯ the royal palace

10. What did the Babylonians do to Jerusalem's walls?   ◯ tore them down   ◯ wrote on them

11. What did the Babylonians do with the people who were still in Jerusalem?
◯ made them join the army   ◯ killed them   ◯ took them away as exiles

12. Imagine that you are a citizen of Judah, living in Jerusalem. For two years, the city has been under siege, surrounded by the Babylonian army. You depend on the king and his army to protect you. Read Jeremiah 52:7. How might you feel about what the king and the army did?

_____

_____

13. Read Jeremiah 52:8. How do you think King Zedekiah felt about his soldiers then? _____

_____

14. What example did King Zedekiah set for his soldiers when he fled from Jerusalem and left the people

unprotected? _____

15. Did his soldiers follow his example? _____

16. What example should King Zedekiah have set? _____

_____

17. Read John 15:13. The person who said these words is Jesus, the King of kings. Compare the example that King Jesus set for us with the example that King Zedekiah set.

_____

_____

_____

_____

18. Which king would you rather depend on if your life was in danger? _____

19. Read Proverbs 17:17. Then read the actions below. Underline the ones that show loyalty.

praying for your friend   HELPING A FRIEND WHO IS IN TROUBLE   MOCKING YOUR FRIEND

hanging out only if your friend is in a good mood   sharing your germs with your friend

being together in good times and bad   playing together only if you are winning the game

sitting together even when other people do not like your friend   sharing your things

20. Describe how you will show loyalty to your friends today.

_____

_____

_____

Mark the statements **T** for true or **F** for false.

_____ **1.** Nehemiah's brother, Hanani, told Nehemiah that all in Jerusalem were doing very well.

_____ **2.** When Nehemiah heard Hanani's report, he cried, prayed, and fasted.

_____ **3.** Nehemiah was afraid to tell King Artaxerxes he was sad because Jerusalem was still in ruins.

_____ **4.** Nehemiah asked King Artaxerxes for send him to Jerusalem to be the governor of Judah.

_____ **5.** When the king heard Nehemiah's request, he granted him permission to return to Jerusalem.

_____ **6.** When Sanballat and Tobiah tried to stop the Israelites, Nehemiah prayed to God for help.

_____ **7.** The people of Judah were confident that they could easily rebuild Jerusalem's walls.

_____ **8.** Nehemiah placed guards with swords, spears, and bows around the wall to protect the workers.

_____ **9.** The workers carried their tools in one hand and their weapons in their other hand.

_____ **10.** It took the people of Judah about 100 days to rebuild the walls of Jerusalem.

11. Rewrite the false sentences so that they are true.

_____

_____

_____

_____

12. Read Nehemiah 8:1–12. Answer the questions.

a. Who read to the people from the platform? _____

b. What did he read? _____

c. How did the people feel they heard what he read? _____

_____

d. What did the governor and priests say to them? _____

_____

e. What had the people understood? _____

_____

13. When Nehemiah encouraged the people, he said the joy of the Lord was their strength. Write three ways you feel the joy of the Lord.

_____

_____

_____

THE
JOY
OF THE
LORD
IS MY
STRENGTH
- NEH 8:10-

14. Write the letter under the picture that most closely matches the action or emotion felt by the person or persons described in each phrase below.

A. How Nehemiah felt when he heard about Jerusalem

B. What Sanballat and Tobiah felt

C. How the Israelites felt when Nehemiah got to Jerusalem

D. How King Artaxerxes felt

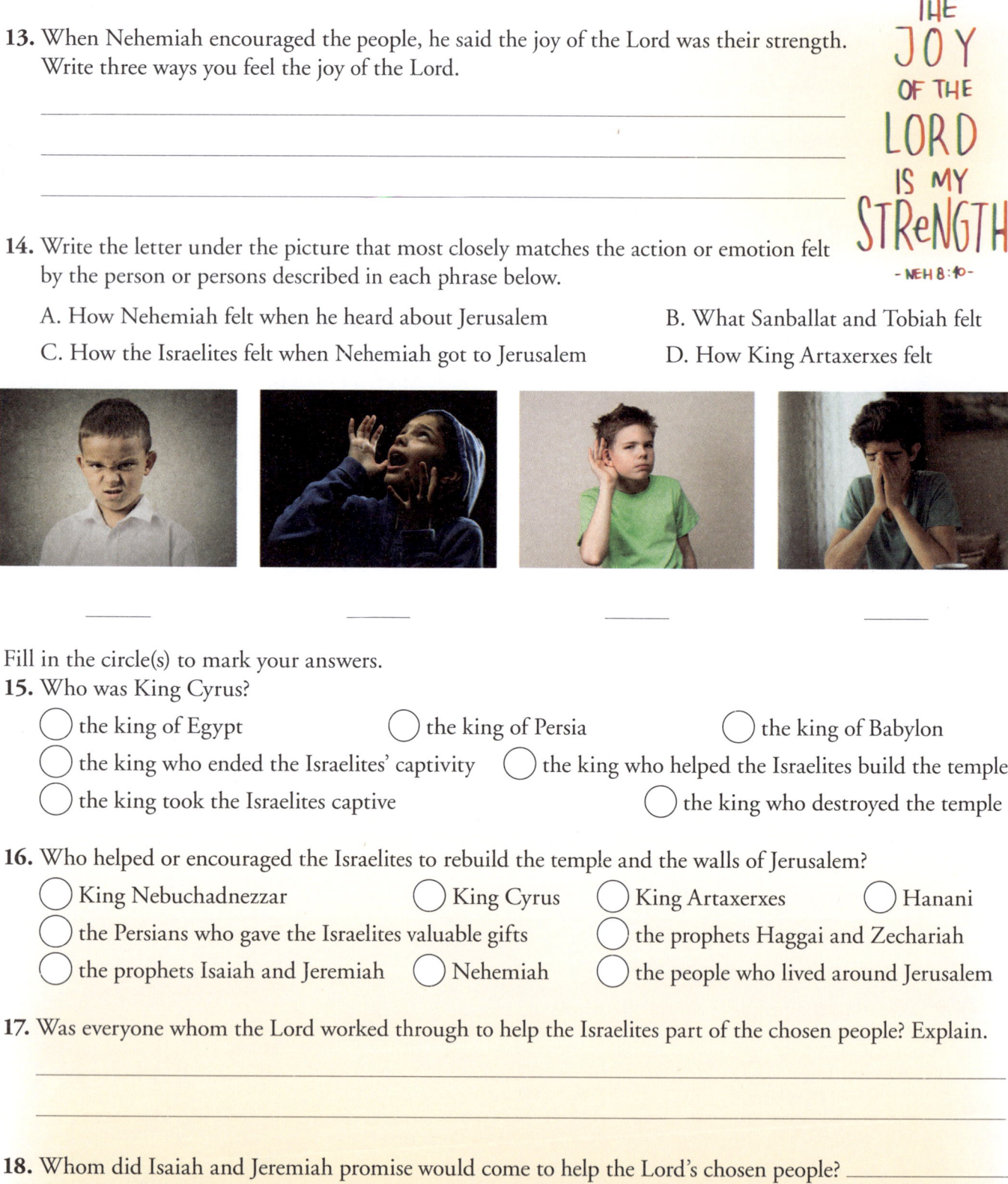

_____   _____   _____   _____

Fill in the circle(s) to mark your answers.

15. Who was King Cyrus?

○ the king of Egypt   ○ the king of Persia   ○ the king of Babylon

○ the king who ended the Israelites' captivity   ○ the king who helped the Israelites build the temple

○ the king took the Israelites captive   ○ the king who destroyed the temple

16. Who helped or encouraged the Israelites to rebuild the temple and the walls of Jerusalem?

○ King Nebuchadnezzar   ○ King Cyrus   ○ King Artaxerxes   ○ Hanani

○ the Persians who gave the Israelites valuable gifts   ○ the prophets Haggai and Zechariah

○ the prophets Isaiah and Jeremiah   ○ Nehemiah   ○ the people who lived around Jerusalem

17. Was everyone whom the Lord worked through to help the Israelites part of the chosen people? Explain.

_____

_____

18. Whom did Isaiah and Jeremiah promise would come to help the Lord's chosen people? _____

_____

19. How long after Jerusalem was rebuilt did their promises come true? _____

_____

1. Write the words of Galatians 4:4–5. Underline the words that will help you memorize the verse.

_____

_____

_____

_____

Match the words from Luke 2 to their descriptions.

2. ____ A feed trough for animals

3. ____ The governor of Syria in the year of Christ's birth

4. ____ A count of the people in a geographic area

| A. Census |
| B. Ancestral |
| C. Descendant |
| D. Quirinius |
| E. Manger |
| F. Firstborn |
| G. Ancient |

5. ____ The oldest child of his or her mother

6. ____ A child, grandchild, great-grandchild, and so on

7. ____ Long ago

8. ____ Related to one's ancestors

9. Read Luke 2:25–32. Answer the questions about Simeon's prophecy.

a. For whom did God prepare salvation? _____

b. What would Jesus bring to the Gentiles? _____

c. Which nation would be glorified through Christ? _____

The wise men offered Jesus three gifts—gold, frankincense and myrrh. Read the paragraph below and answer the questions on the next page.

The gifts of from the wise men signified who Jesus was as well as what he would do for us. Gold signified royalty, an appropriate gift for one king to give to another because of its beauty and usefulness. Frankincense was associated with holiness, and in the temple, it was burned, creating a pleasant aroma for God. Myrrh symbolized Jesus' sacrifice for sin. It is a spice that was used to prepare bodies for burial. Nicodemus brought spices, including myrrh, to prepare Jesus' body for burial.

10. Which gift was appropriate for Jesus as King of kings? _____

11. Which gift was significant because Jesus died and was laid in a tomb? _____

12. Which gift symbolizes Jesus' holiness and his deity as the Son of God? _____

13. Which gift did Nicodemus bring to prepare Jesus' body for burial? _____

14. Which gift has the greatest value today? _____

15. Jesus was truly God and truly human at the same time. He showed his dual nature when he was in the temple at the age of 12. Read the passages listed. Tell how it applies to either Jesus' divinity or humanity. The first one is done for you.

Scripture	Jesus' Divinity	Jesus' Humanity
Luke 2:49	He was in his Father's (God's) house.	
John 11:35		
Mark 9:2–3		
Matthew 8:24		
Luke 24:41–43		

16. Joseph, Jesus' earthly father, was a carpenter. It was the Jewish custom for fathers to teach their sons the same profession they followed, so Jesus probably learned carpentry too. Carpenters cut and shape wood into useful objects. What gifts and talents do you have and what might you produce with your life?

_____

_____

_____

_____

_____

1. The puzzle below contains a sentence about baptism. Use pencil to complete the puzzle by entering letters into the boxes. Once you've entered a letter, cross it off the list below. Do not write heavily because you may have a mistake that you have to erase later on. Use the hints below.

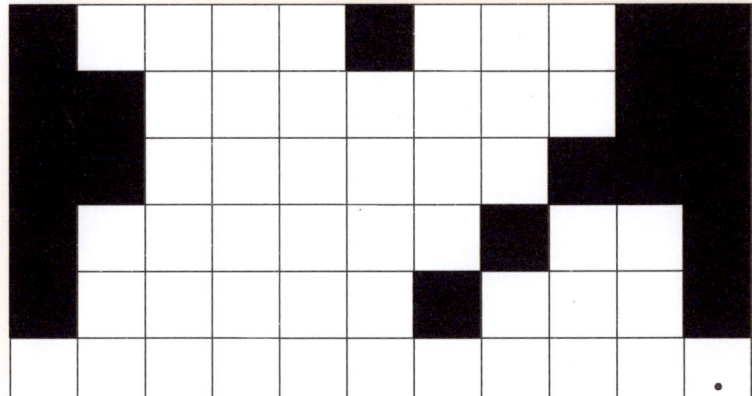

Hints:
Jesus' cousin

past tense of call

human beings

trust in God

the act of expressing regret for sin

**Letters in the puzzle: B, H, P, C, A, P, L, A, D, E, E, O, I, T, H, I, A, C
J, P, O, N, T, E, N, T, E, P, A, A, N, T, E, S, N, O, R, F, E, E, L, L, T, H, T, D**

Read the Bible verses. Match Jesus' response to Satan's temptations.

2. _____ Jesus was tempted to turn stones into bread.

3. _____ Jesus was tempted to prove his divinity by jumping from the highest point of the temple.

| A. Deuteronomy 6:16 |
| B. Deuteronomy 8:3 |
| C. Deuteronomy 6:13 |

4. _____ He was tempted to gain all the kingdoms of the world if he would worship Satan.

5. Read Hebrews 4:15. Answer the questions.

a. What is Jesus' role as described in the verse? _____

b. In what way was Jesus like we are? _____

c. Did Jesus give in to temptation or testing? _____

d. What can believers do to resist temptation? _____

_____

Read Luke 4:17–21 in your Student Textbook. Answer the riddles. You can use the same answer more than once.

6. Who am I? I read the Scripture in my hometown of Nazareth. _____

7. Who am I? I wrote the prophecy that Jesus read in the synagogue. _____

8. Who are we? The Savior will bring good news to us. _____

9. Who are we? The Savior will come to set us free. _____

10. Who are we? The Savior will come to help us see. _____

11. Who am I? I fulfilled the prophecy and announced it to the people in the synagogue in Nazareth.

_____

Jesus called 12 disciples. Fill in the circle that describes what each disciple was before following Jesus.

12. Peter

◯ tax collector ◯ fisherman ◯ zealot

13. Matthew

◯ tax collector ◯ shepherd ◯ fisherman

14. James, son of Zebedee

◯ soldier ◯ shepherd ◯ fisherman

15. John, James' brother

◯ carpenter ◯ fisherman ◯ cook

16. Andrew, Peter's brother

◯ fisherman ◯ shepherd ◯ sailor

17. Simon

◯ zealot ◯ priest ◯ clerk

18. God can use people in all professions to serve him to "fish for people." Fishing for people means to tell others about Christ and how to be saved. Write 3 or 4 sentences about how you can help people know Jesus as their Savior. _____

_____

_____

_____

_____

_____

1. Complete the definition of born again.

Being born again is a _____ birth into God's

_____ through _____ in Christ

and the _____ of the _____

_____ .

2. When the Holy Spirit indwells believers, he imparts a variety of blessings. Read each verse. Write **teach**, **power**, **truth**, **preaching**, **spiritual rebirth**, or **fruit** on the line as it applies to the verse.

a. Galatians 5:22 _____

b. Luke 12:12 _____

c. John 3:6 _____

d. John 14:17 _____

e. Luke 24:49 _____

f. Acts 4:31 _____

3. Jesus taught that discipleship requires commitment. Read the statements below. Rewrite each statement so that it agrees with Christ's teaching.

I don't need to listen to God's Word.

I will obey a few of God's commands.

Putting God first isn't important for disciples.

I will always love my family more than God.

I'll follow Jesus when it's convenient.

I can follow Jesus without giving up my own plans.

a. _____

b. _____

c. _____

d. _____

e. _____

f. _____

Read each comment. Write **God** or **money**, depending on who or what seems to be the speaker's master.

4. _____ "I'll give an offering if I have anything left over from my allowance."

5. _____ "Poor people should get jobs. Why should I donate to meet their needs?"

6. _____ "I only have five dollars, but I'll give it to someone who needs it."

7. _____ "God expects us to give our time to the church, not our cash."

8. In Jesus' parable of the Good Samaritan, several people saw the injured man. Reread the parable, found in Luke 10:25–37. How do you think each person in the story would answer the questions?

	Priest	Temple Assistant	Samaritan
Should I see if the man is okay?			
Do I have a responsibility to serve those in need?			
If serving people means I have to spend my own money, should I help?			
Why should I serve someone who might not thank me or return the favor?			
What will people think of me if I serve this injured man?			

1. Read your memory verse, Galatians 4:4–5. Answer the questions.

   a. Who sent Jesus to Earth?

   _____

   b. What was Jesus' purpose in coming to Earth? _____

   _____

   _____

   c. Why was God the Son the only one who could purchase our freedom from sin? _____

   _____

2. Jesus is 100% God and 100% human. Place a check mark in front of the ways Jesus proved that he is God the Son.

   _____ Jesus cast out demons.   _____ Jesus healed the sick.

   _____ Jesus spoke to the temple leaders.   _____ Jesus chose disciples.

   _____ Jesus learned carpentry.   _____ Jesus forgave sins.

   _____ Jesus lived in Nazareth.   _____ Jesus fulfilled Isaiah's prophecy.

Jesus, God the Son, has power over all evil. He sent the demons into the pigs and freed the demon-possessed man. Read the verses and the questions. Fill in the circle(s) of all correct answers.

3. In Ephesians 6:12, whom does Paul say our battle is against?

   ◯ flesh and blood enemies   ◯ evil spirits
   ◯ evil rulers in the unseen world   ◯ other nations

4. In Romans 8:38, what can separate us from God's love?

   ◯ demons   ◯ powers of hell
   ◯ nothing   ◯ angels

5. In Ephesians 2:2, who or what did believers follow before they came to faith in Christ?

   ◯ the devil   ◯ their earthly leaders
   ◯ prophets   ◯ angels

6. Jesus proved that he is God the Son by demonstrating his authority over nature. Use the Word Bank to complete the sentences. You may use words more than once.

Word Bank				
pray	terrified	faith	waves	ghost

Jesus often spent time alone to _____. One evening, he sent his disciples across the Sea of Galilee in a small boat. Jesus himself was not with them. Night fell, but the disciples were far from shore. A storm arose and the sea became rough. High _____ threatened the boat. About three o'clock in the morning, the disciples thought they saw a _____ walking toward them on the sea. They were _____. The man walking toward them was not a ghost; it was Jesus! When Peter saw Jesus, he asked if he might join him on the water. As long as Peter kept his eyes on Jesus, he, too, walked on the sea. But when Peter noticed the choppy _____ and felt the strong wind, he was _____. Then Jesus reached out and saved him. He said to Peter, "You have so little _____. Why did you doubt me?"

7. Read Luke 7:11–17. Underline the words that describe Jesus and his miracle in this passage.

compassionate	powerful	uncaring	active
mighty	lazy	able	ill
incapable	strong	bored	weak
merciful	concerned	silly	quiet

Read Matthew 17:1–9. Choose and underline the best word to complete each sentence.

8. Jesus took Peter, James, and John up to a high (mountain, ravine) to be alone.

9. Jesus' appearance was (concerned, transformed) so that his face (shone, reflected) like the sun.

10. While the disciples watched, Moses and Elijah (entered, appeared) and spoke with (Jesus, God).

11. Peter wanted to build (five, three) shelters for Jesus, Moses, and Elijah.

12. God the Father spoke and told the disciples to (preach, listen) to Jesus.

Refer to Topic 5 in your Student Textbook. Identify each statement as **true** or **false**. Write the reference from Matthew, Mark, or John that supports your answer.

1. _____ Judas betrayed Jesus to the Roman leaders.

_____

2. _____ Jesus entered Jerusalem humbly, riding a donkey.

_____

3. _____ The people of Jerusalem shouted, "Blessings on the one who comes in the name of the Lord!"

_____

4. _____ The entire city of Jerusalem was cheering. The crowds called Jesus the Messiah from Bethlehem in Judea.

_____

5. _____ After supper, Jesus explained that the bread represented his body and the wine represented his blood.

_____

6. _____ Jesus was on trial before Pontius Pilate, the Roman chief of police.

_____

7. _____ The Romans hung a sign on Jesus' cross that told everyone his name.

_____

8. _____ Jesus was crucified along with two other innocent men.

_____

9. _____ Jesus said that his work on Earth was finished. Then he bowed his head and died.

_____

_____

10. Read Matthew 27:51–53. Number the events that occurred after Jesus' death on the cross in the order of Matthew's presentation.

_____ Tombs opened.

_____ The bodies of many holy people who had died were raised to life.

_____ The curtain of the temple was torn in two from top to bottom.

_____ The earth shook.

11. People held different opinions as to Jesus' identity as God the Son. Some had faith, but others had folly (foolishness). Read the statements and determine if they show the speaker's faith or folly. Write an **X** in the correct column.

	Faith	Folly
The crowd waved branches and yelled, "Praise God for the Son of David. Blessings on the one who comes in the name of the Lord!"		
The Roman officer said, "This man truly was the Son of God!"		
The people said, "He saved others; let him save himself."		
A bystander said, "Wait. Let's see whether Elijah comes to take him down!"		
The leading priests and teachers of religious law also mocked Jesus. "He saved others," they scoffed, "but he can't save himself!		
The people passing by shouted abuse, shaking their heads in mockery. "Ha! Look at you now!" they yelled at him. "You said you were going to destroy the Temple and rebuild it in three days. Well then, save yourself and come down from the cross!"		

Who do you say Jesus is? Read each statement. Write **I agree** or **I disagree** on the line.

12. _____ Jesus was a wise person, but he was just a man.

13. _____ Jesus was a good teacher but nothing more than that.

14. _____ Jesus is the Son of God, the Savior of the world.

15. _____ Jesus is the Messiah, the Lord's chosen Savior

16. _____ Jesus was a revolutionary who deserved to die.

17. _____ Jesus is my Lord and Savior.

18. _____ Jesus was a special human being, but he was not God.

19. Pontius Pilate responded to the pleas of the mob and released Barabbas, the revolutionary and murderer, instead of Jesus. Have you ever done something that you knew was wrong because everyone else was doing it? Tell about your experience.

_____

_____

1. Read Galatians 4:4–5. Answer the questions.

a. When did God send his Son? _____

b. How was Jesus the same as we are? _____

c. What was Jesus' mission? _____

2. Read John 20:1–18 and Matthew 28:11–15. Number the sentences in the correct order to tell the events of Jesus' resurrection.

_____ Mary Magdalene and others went to Jesus' tomb while it was still dark.

_____ Mary Magdalene told the disciples that she had seen Jesus.

_____ Peter and John ran to the tomb.

_____ Peter saw the linen cloths lying where Jesus had lain.

_____ Before Mary and the other women arrived at the tomb, the stone had been moved.

_____ Mary told Peter and John that Jesus' body was gone.

_____ Mary saw a person who she thought was the gardener.

_____ That evening, the disciples met behind locked doors out of fear.

_____ John reached the tomb first.

3. Complete the definition of the Great Commission.

Jesus' _____ to all _____ to preach the _____ , to _____ new believers, and to teach all the _____ of Christ.

4. Check the ways you can help the church to fulfill the Great Commission.

I can live out the Great Commission by . . .

_____ giving someone a Bible   _____ telling people about Jesus   _____ going camping

_____ visiting another country   _____ learning Jesus' commands   _____ avoiding people

_____ making fun of someone's false worldview   _____ diligently praying for missionaries

_____ telling people how smart I am   _____ inviting a friend to come to church with me

_____ telling little kids to obey me   _____ sharing God's Word   _____ being kind

Match the key people, places, and events of Jesus' crucifixion and resurrection with their description.

5. _____ Pontius Pilate

6. _____ Judas

7. _____ Joseph of Arimathea

8. _____ The Lord's Supper

9. _____ The Mount of Olives

10. _____ Simon Peter

11. _____ John

12. _____ The Passover Lamb

> A. Jesus, the sacrifice for our sins
> B. The place of Jesus' ascension
> C. The disciple who went into the tomb
> D. The Roman governor of Judea
> E. The name of the meal instituting a new covenant between God and people
> F. The Pharisee who asked Pilate for Jesus' body
> G. The disciple who outran Peter
> H. The disciple who betrayed Jesus

Fill in the circle that tells the reason for each action.

13. Jesus described the bread and wine of the Passover Feast as his body and blood.
○ to begin a new covenant   ○ to start a tradition   ○ to do away with the past

14. Jesus died on the cross.
○ to pay for his sins   ○ to pay for our sins   ○ to follow the Law of Moses

15. Pontius Pilate released a criminal, Barabbas, instead of Jesus.
○ to let an innocent man go   ○ to scold the Jewish leaders   ○ to please the people

16. Jesus appeared after the resurrection.
○ to unlock the doors   ○ to check on Judas   ○ to encourage the disciples

17. Jesus gave the Great Commission.
○ to leave parting words   ○ to overcome sin   ○ to give us an assignment

18. Think about how the world would be different if Jesus had not come to Earth, died for our sins, and risen again. Write three sentences telling about how life would be different.

_____

_____

_____

_____

Getting Started and Topics 1 and 2

1. According to your memory verse, whom did Jesus say would help his followers to be his witnesses?

_____

2. Where would they tell others about him? _____

_____

Match the term to its meaning.

_____ **3.** Church

_____ **4.** Witness

_____ **5.** Testify

A. Someone with personal knowledge about a specific matter

B. To share personal knowledge or belief or provide evidence or proof

C. People who profess faith in Christ

Mark the statements below with a **T** if they are true or with an **F** if they are false.

_____ **6.** The Roman Empire extended from Europe to the Middle East and North Africa.

_____ **7.** Jerusalem was the capital of the Roman Empire.

_____ **8.** The people of the Roman Empire only spoke Romanian.

_____ **9.** In the first century, most boys and girls were taught by their parents at home.

_____ **10.** Children were not allowed to work on farms, in gardens, or in their parents' places of business.

_____ **11.** Most people lived in small villages and in the countryside.

_____ **12.** The Romans built roads to help soldiers and tradespeople travel throughout the empire.

_____ **13.** Many gods and goddesses were worshipped in the Roman Empire.

_____ **14.** Archeology helps us discover how people lived in Bible times.

15. Rewrite the false sentences so that they are true.

_____

_____

_____

_____

Circle the correct word(s) or number to complete each statement below.

16. The Bible is a collection of (66 / 27) books by many different writers inspired by God.

17. Acts was written about (100 / 30 / 2) years after Jesus' death on the cross.

18. Acts is the shortened title of The Acts of the (Hebrews / Apostles / Romans).

19. Acts is a (historical / fictional) record that tells how the church began.

20. The good news the disciples shared was for (Israelites only / everyone).

21. Some people thought that the followers of Jesus were (crazy about crosses / criminals).

22. Acts reminded believers in the first century of all (Peter / Paul / the Holy Spirit) had done among them.

23. Write about a time that someone shared their personal knowledge of Jesus with you. _____

_____

_____

_____

24. Write about a time when you shared your faith with someone else.

_____

_____

_____

_____

_____

25. What might help you share about Jesus more often? _____

_____

_____

_____

Fill in the circle(s) to answer each question.

1. What was Luke's profession?   ◯ soldier   ◯ doctor   ◯ carpenter

2. What was Luke known for in the first century church?

◯ He was Jesus' cousin.   ◯ He traveled with Paul telling others about Jesus.

◯ He was the first person arrested for praying in public.

◯ He had been raised from the dead.   ◯ He was Jesus' brother.

3. What did Luke write?   ◯ poetry   ◯ history   ◯ biography

4. Which books did Luke write?

◯ Luke and Philippians   ◯ Luke and Revelation   ◯ Luke and Acts   ◯ Luke and Romans

5. How did Luke go about writing his books?

◯ He had visions and wrote down what he saw.   ◯ He took dictation from Paul in prison.

◯ He did research and interviewed eyewitnesses.   ◯ He made them up.

6. Why did Luke write?

◯ to tell people about Jesus and how the church grew   ◯ to pass the time in prison

◯ to show that Jesus' followers were not troublemakers   ◯ to encourage those who trust in Christ

7. What kind of writer was Luke?

◯ He only wrote about important events.   ◯ He paid attention to details.

◯ He only wrote about himself or other men.   ◯ He was humble and focused on others.

8. What cities did Luke visit?

◯ Antioch, Philippi, Ephesus, and Rome   ◯ Bethlehem, Nazareth, and Jerusalem

9. Read the Bible verses from the gospel of Luke. Match them to the illustration.

A. Luke 8:22–25   B. Luke 2:39–40   C. Luke 8:40–42, 49–56

_____   _____   _____

10. Each letter in Luke's name can stand for something about who he was. Write a sentence to explain how you know that Luke showed at least one of the qualities listed after each letter.

L – loving, loyal, listener: _____
_____
_____

U – understanding, upbeat: _____
_____
_____

K – knowledgeable, kind: _____
_____
_____

E – evangelist, educated, expressive: _____
_____
_____

11. Which of the above qualities would you like people to think of when they think about you? Why?
_____
_____

12. Write your name or initials. Choose words that begin with those letters to tell who you are.

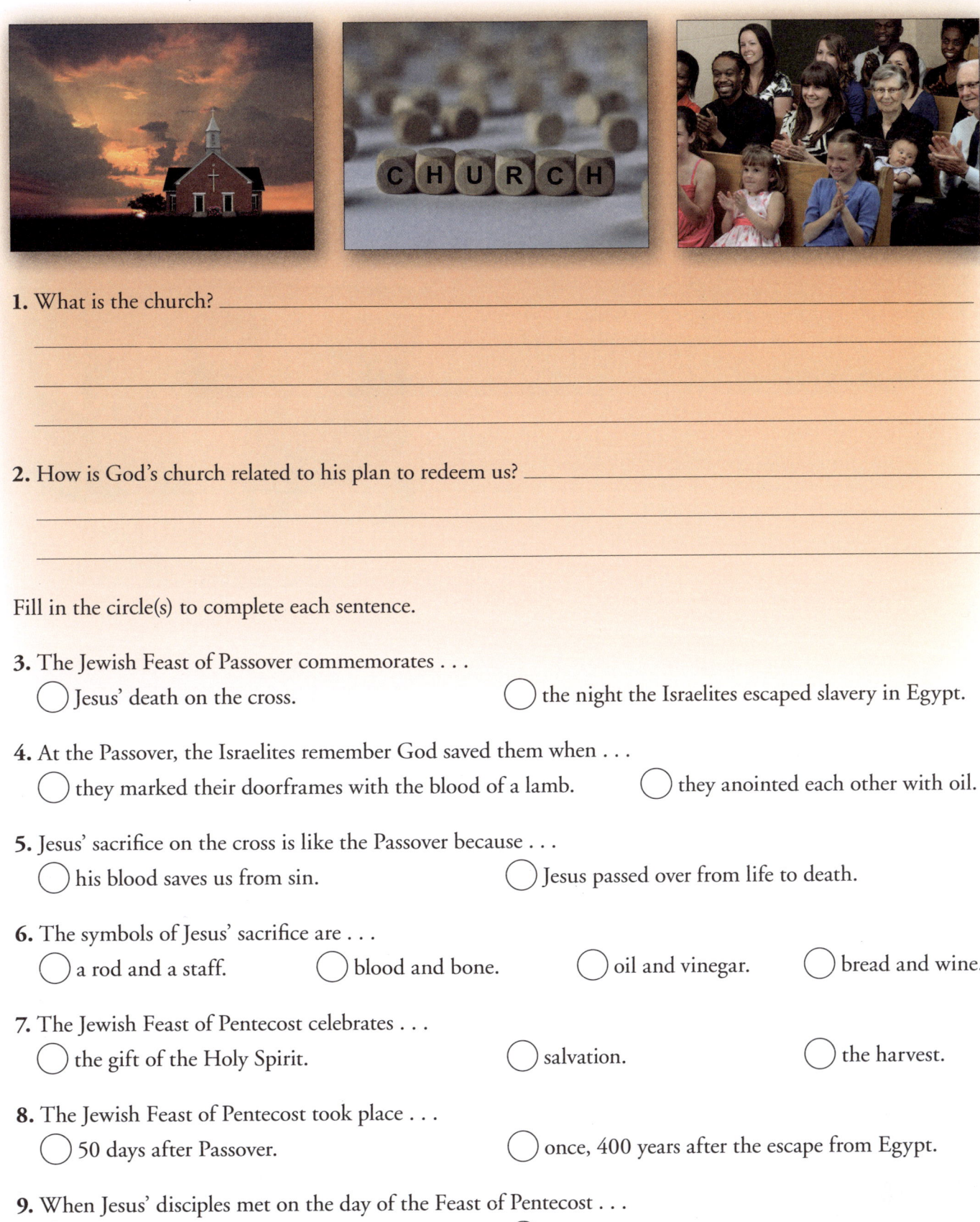

1. What is the church? _____

_____

_____

_____

2. How is God's church related to his plan to redeem us? _____

_____

_____

Fill in the circle(s) to complete each sentence.

3. The Jewish Feast of Passover commemorates . . .

◯ Jesus' death on the cross.　　　　◯ the night the Israelites escaped slavery in Egypt.

4. At the Passover, the Israelites remember God saved them when . . .

◯ they marked their doorframes with the blood of a lamb.　　◯ they anointed each other with oil.

5. Jesus' sacrifice on the cross is like the Passover because . . .

◯ his blood saves us from sin.　　　　◯ Jesus passed over from life to death.

6. The symbols of Jesus' sacrifice are . . .

◯ a rod and a staff.　　◯ blood and bone.　　◯ oil and vinegar.　　◯ bread and wine.

7. The Jewish Feast of Pentecost celebrates . . .

◯ the gift of the Holy Spirit.　　◯ salvation.　　◯ the harvest.

8. The Jewish Feast of Pentecost took place . . .

◯ 50 days after Passover.　　◯ once, 400 years after the escape from Egypt.

9. When Jesus' disciples met on the day of the Feast of Pentecost . . .

◯ Jesus ascended to heaven.　　◯ the Holy Spirit came, and the church was born.

10. After his resurrection, what did Jesus command his disciples to be? _____

_____

11. What did he promise that would help them do this? _____

12. How did the disciples know Jesus' promise was fulfilled? _____

_____

_____

13. Peter explained these events to the crowd. From your memory verse, what did Peter say people needed to do to be forgiven of their sins? _____

_____

_____

14. What would the people who did this receive?

_____

Complete the table below.

	Bible Verse	What Believers Receive from The Holy Spirit
15.	Acts 1:8	
16.	Romans 8:14–16	
17.	Romans 15:13	
18.	1 Corinthians 2:12	
19.	1 Corinthians 12:7–11	
20.	Galatians 6:8	
21.	Ephesians 3:16	
22.	1 Thessalonians 1:6	

23. Write the words to Acts 2:38. _____

_____

_____

_____

_____

Match each phrase about Jesus' ascension into heaven to the Scripture verse where it is found.

A. Acts 1:11   B. Acts 1:9   C. Acts 1:5

D. Acts 1:4   E. Acts 1:8

_____ **1.** The command Jesus gave the disciples after his resurrection

_____ **2.** The gift Jesus promised his disciples would receive

_____ **3.** What Jesus' disciples would become

_____ **4.** What happened after Jesus spoke

_____ **5.** The promise the two white-robed men made

6. What might have you felt if you had been with the disciples when Jesus ascended

to heaven? _____

_____

_____

7. Read 1 Thessalonians 4:16–18. Answer the questions.

a. What will the Lord Jesus' return will be like? _____

_____

_____

b. How is the thought of Jesus' return an encouragement to you and to other believers?

_____

_____

_____

8. What important things should you do while you wait for Jesus to return? Circle your choices.

read your Bible   protect endangered animals   travel the world nonstop   go shopping

stop working   hide in an underground bunker   go to church   do good to everyone

watch television   tell people about Jesus   love your family and community   pray

party all the time   clean up the environment   avoid people who are not believers

worship God   work hard   enjoy and take care of the people and things around you

live to please only yourself   live to please only others   worship material blessings

Answer the questions below about who the disciples chose to replace Judas.

9. Who were the 11 disciples Jesus told to wait in Jerusalem for the Holy Spirit?

_____

_____

10. Explain how Judas' death and his replacement were foretold.

_____

_____

11. What requirements did Peter say the man who would replace Judas must have?

_____

_____

12. What did the apostles ask God to do before they cast lots to choose a new apostle?

_____

_____

13. Whom did God choose to be the new apostle? _____

Read the sentences. Mark them **T** for true or **F** for false.

_____ **14.** For 40 days after he rose again, Jesus appeared to the apostles from time to time.

_____ **15.** Jesus talked to the apostles about the kingdom of God.

_____ **16.** The apostles waited in Jerusalem for the Holy Spirit Jesus had promised.

_____ **17.** The apostles waited all alone.

_____ **18.** All believers in Christ are apostles.

19. Rewrite the false sentences so that they are true.

_____

_____

_____

1. Everyone in the city is talking about some very strange events that took place about nine o'clock on the morning of the Pentecost feast. What happened?

_____

_____

_____

2. My father's friend told him he thought the Galilean disciples were drunk. Then he said the apostle Peter got up and explained that what was happening was the fulfillment of some prophecy. Were they really drunk? Who was the prophet he was talking about and what he had prophesied? _____

_____

_____

3. Everyone is still talking about the man named *Jesus* who was crucified a few weeks ago. Some people even say he came back to life. What did Peter say about Jesus?

_____

_____

_____

4. How did the people respond to Peter's message about Jesus? What did they do?

_____

_____

_____

Underline the correct answers.

5. On whom did God promise to pour out his Spirit?

all people   young women   old women   young men   daughters   old men   sons

6. Whom did Peter say the promise was for?

only those in the crowd that day   everyone who is called by God

the people in the crowd, their children, and people far away   the crooked generation

7. What would people do when they received the Spirit?

drink   dance   dream   laugh   cry   prophesy   see visions

Match the verses to each picture.

A. John 15:5   B. Matthew 9:37–38   C. 1 Corinthians 15:20
D. James 5:7   E. Revelation 14:16   F. Matthew 13:23

8. _____

9. _____

10. _____

11. _____

12. _____

13. _____

Use the Word Bank to complete the sentences. Some words are used more than once.

| Word Bank |
| harvest   church   possession   foretaste |

14. The Holy Spirit within us is a _____ of future glory.

15. We are God the Father's prized _____ in all of creation.

16. Jesus is the first of a great _____ of all who have died.

17. The harvest of those who believe and are baptized in Jesus' name is the _____.

18. The _____ at Pentecost was more than 3,000 new believers.

19. The believers joyfully shared every _____ they had, including money and property.

20. The _____ includes everyone who believes in Jesus.

21. How has the message of Pentecost changed your life? _____

_____

_____

Getting Started and Topic 1

1. Write the words of your memory verse, Acts 5:29. Highlight Peter's words.

_____

_____

_____

Match each action with the reason for the action.

2. _____ The apostles preached to the people of Jerusalem . . .

3. _____ Peter and John went to the temple . . .

4. _____ The lame man was carried to the temple gate . . .

5. _____ The man begged Peter, John, and others for money . . .

6. _____ The crowds in the temple were astounded . . .

7. _____ The man's feet and ankles were strengthened. He jumped up, stood on his feet, and began to walk . . .

A. because Peter healed him in Jesus' name.

B. because he was lame in his feet and ankles and couldn't walk.

C. because Jesus commanded the disciples to be his witnesses to Jerusalem, all Judea, Samaria, and to the ends of the earth.

D. because they saw that the lame man had been healed.

E. because he could not earn money by working for a living.

F. because they wanted to take part in the three o'clock prayer service.

8. Read the verses. On the line, write the words that are the same in each verse.

a. 1 Corinthians 6:11   b. Ephesians 5:20   c. Philippians 2:10

_____

9. Read Acts 3:4–6, 16. Answer the questions.

a. In whose name was the lame man healed? _____

b. In whom did the crippled man place his faith? _____

c. Did Peter heal in his own name or in the name of Jesus? _____

d. Why do you think it is important to treat the name of Jesus with respect? _____

_____

Use the Word Bank to complete the sentences.

Word Bank			
rejected	faith	repenting	Messiah
ignorance	covenant	prophet	power

10. Peter explained that he had not healed the lame man through his own _____.

11. The lame man's _____ in the name of Jesus healed him.

12. The people of Jerusalem _____ Jesus and killed the Author of Life.

13. What the people did to Jesus was done in _____.

14. Starting with Samuel, every _____ said that the Messiah must suffer.

15. Peter explained that God would again send Jesus, the appointed _____.

16. In fulfillment of God's _____, all families on Earth would be blessed.

17. The people would be blessed by turning back from their sins and _____.

18. Peter's sermon included reminders of fulfilled prophecy as well as promises for the people. Read each statement and make an **X** in the correct column.

	Fulfilled Prophecy	Promise
The Messiah must suffer for sins of the people.		
Jesus, the Messiah, will come again.		
Through Abraham's descendants, all the families of Earth would be blessed.		
God will bless those who repent and turn away from their sinful ways.		
Jesus will remain in heaven until the time for the final restoration of all things.		

19. The healing of the crippled man gave Peter an opportunity to tell others about Jesus. Write two sentences about an opportunity you have had to share your faith with someone else.

_____

1. Read the statements. Write a **P** if it is a belief of the Pharisees and an **S** if it is a belief of the Sadducees.

_____ There is no life after death.   _____ No one will be bodily resurrected.   _____ Jesus was not raised.

_____ Heaven is a real place.   _____ Life ends with death.   _____ There is life after death.

_____ People who believe and trust in God will have eternal life.   _____ Nothing exists after death.

_____ Those who do good works will be rewarded in the afterlife.

Fill in the circle(s) to answer to each question.

2. By what power was the lame man healed?

◯ by his own power   ◯ by the powerful name of Jesus

◯ by a super power   ◯ by Peter's divine power

3. In whose name was the man healed?

◯ in Peter's name   ◯ in Jesus' name

◯ in John's name   ◯ in the name of the gospel

4. Who or what was "the stone that the builders rejected"?

◯ the high council   ◯ Jesus   ◯ Peter and John   ◯ the keystone

5. What did the high council notice about Peter and John?

◯ their fame   ◯ their boldness   ◯ their special training in the Scriptures

6. When the council could not decide what to do with the apostles, what did they do?

◯ fed them   ◯ praised them   ◯ warned them   ◯ believed them

7. Whom did Peter and John say they must obey?

◯ the high council   ◯ God   ◯ the other apostles   ◯ no one

8. After Peter and John were released, they gathered for prayer with other believers. Make a check mark in front of the requests the church made in their prayer.

_____ great boldness   _____ punishment for the high council members   _____ forgiveness

_____ healing power   _____ miraculous signs and wonders   _____ good plans

_____ silver and gold   _____ more persecution and threats   _____ earthquakes

9. Read Acts 4:32–37 and Acts 5:1–11. Determine if each action encouraged or discouraged the growth and unity of the Jerusalem church. Write an **X** in the correct column.

	Encouraged the Church	Discouraged the Church
Believers were united in heart and mind.		
Believers shared everything they had.		
Barnabas sold a field and gave the money to the apostles.		
Ananias brought part of the money he had received to the disciples, but he kept back some money.		
Sapphira lied to Peter.		
There were no needy people in the church because those who owned land sold it and shared the money.		
Ananias lied to God.		
Great fear gripped the people when they heard of Ananias' and Sapphira's deaths. It showed the church that God is serious about sin.		

10. Read 2 Corinthians 9:7. Answer the questions.

a. How should Christians determine how much to give to the church? _____

_____

b. How shouldn't they give? _____

c. If you choose to give, what should your attitude be?

_____

_____

d. What was wrong with the way Ananias and Sapphira chose to give to the church? _____

_____

11. Have you ever given to others? Tell about what you gave and to whom you gave it. Explain why your gift was important.

_____

_____

_____

1. Number the pictures in the order they occurred in the book of Acts.

_____

Peter said that the apostles must obey God rather than human authority.

_____

Gamaliel advised the high council to leave the apostles alone.

_____

An angel of the Lord let the apostles out of jail at night.

_____

Crowds came from villages all around, bringing sick people to the apostles, and the sick were healed.

_____

The captain of the temple guard and the leading priests did not understand how the apostles could have vanished from a securely locked jail.

_____

After the angel set them free, Peter and John returned to the temple and immediately began preaching.

2. Read Peter's words in Acts 5:29. Answer the questions.

a. Whom did Peter say he must obey? _____

b. Which authority is greater—human authority or God's authority? _____

c. If a human authority tells you to do something that is against God's Word, what must you do?

_____

_____

3. Peter, John, and the other apostles continued to preach in the name of Jesus. What was their message? To learn it, use the code below.

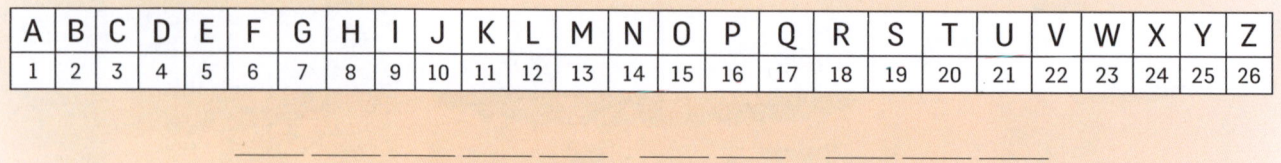

A	B	C	D	E	F	G	H	I	J	K	L	M	N	O	P	Q	R	S	T	U	V	W	X	Y	Z
1	2	3	4	5	6	7	8	9	10	11	12	13	14	15	16	17	18	19	20	21	22	23	24	25	26

___ ___ ___ ___ ___   ___ ___   ___ ___ ___
10 5 19 21 19   9 19   20 8 5

___ ___ ___ ___ ___ ___ ___ .
13 5 19 19 9 1 8

Read the statements below. Write **T** if the statement truthfully reflects Gamaliel's wise advice. Write **U** if it is untrue.

4. _____ "Put the men in jail. If you do not, they will continue to preach in Jesus' name."

5. _____ "Send the men out of the city. Their followers will leave Jerusalem in peace."

6. _____ "Leave the men alone. If they are doing these things on their own, it will be overthrown."

7. _____ "These men cannot speak for God. You will be able to overthrow this new movement."

8. _____ "Let the men go. If their message is from God, you may find yourselves fighting God."

9. _____ "Kill these men. That will stop this nonsense about resurrection and everlasting life."

10. _____ "Kill the men who were with Jesus. The rest of the believers will scatter."

Read the following scenarios. Then write wise, godly advice on the lines below.

11. Olivia's friend thinks it's funny to post jokes about other students online. She wants Olivia to do the same, but Olivia is not so sure it is right to do. What advice would you have for her?

_____

_____

_____

12. Nathan's friends think it is cool to swear and use Jesus' name to cuss. They think Nathan is too righteous to be a friend because he refuses to talk this way, so they don't want to be around him. What advice would you give Nathan? _____

_____

_____

_____

Getting Started and Topic 1   20.1

1. Read Romans 1:16 and write the words on the lines. _____

_____

_____

2. Fill in the blanks to complete the definition of a deacon.

A _____ of the _____ who is _____ by the

_____ to _____ certain _____

Read Acts 6:1–7 and the statements below. Write **T** for true and **F** for false. Rewrite the false statements to make them true.

3. _____ The Greek and Hebrew widows were treated equally in regard to food distribution.

_____

_____

4. _____ The Greek believers saw that their widows were discriminated against.

_____

5. _____ The apostles decided not to bother with such a trivial problem.

_____

6. _____ The apostles prayerfully considered and chose seven godly men to serve as deacons.

_____

7. _____ Stephen was one of the deacons.

_____

8. _____ Peter, John, and the other apostles worked to distribute food.

_____

9. _____ Because the church chose deacons, the apostles could devote themselves to prayer.

_____

10. _____ The apostles commissioned deacons by laying their hands on them.

_____

11. Read Paul's instructions for deacons in 1 Timothy 3:8–13 and answer the questions.

a. What must church deacons be? _____

_____

b. What must they not be? _____

c. How should a deacon treat his family members?

_____

_____

d. How should deacons' wives behave?

_____

_____

_____

e. What reward will a deacon receive? _____

_____

_____

12. Read Acts 6:3–8. Underline Stephen's qualifications to be a deacon.

wise	25 YEARS OLD	had a beard	**full of the Spirit**	EDUCATED
wealthy	*willing to serve*	**athletic**	able to speak Greek	lived nearby

well-known or well-respected   tall and handsome   able to speak Hebrew

13. Most churches today have deacons although they may not be known by that name. Place a check mark next to the possible duties of deacons in modern churches.

_____ collect offerings   _____ help in Sunday school   _____ serve communion

_____ preach sermons   _____ lead worship singing   _____ visit the sick

_____ maintain church grounds   _____ drink coffee before service   _____ manage finances

_____ serve on committees   _____ go overseas as missionaries   _____ run for office

14. Write about the various duties that people do for your church. Include things that you can do to help others. _____

_____

_____

1. Read the apostle Paul's words in Romans 1:16. Answer the questions.

  a. Is Paul embarrassed or ashamed because of the gospel of Christ? _____

  b. What power does faith in Jesus have? _____

  c. How do you know that salvation is for all people? _____

  _____

2. Number the pictures in the order they occurred in the book of Acts.

_____

As they stoned him, Stephen prayed, "Lord, Jesus, receive my spirit."

_____

Using very strong language, Stephen accused the Jews of killing Jesus.

_____

Some men lied about Stephen, saying, "We heard him blaspheme Moses, and even God."

_____

Stephen, a man full of God's grace and power, performed amazing miracles and signs among the people.

_____

So they arrested Stephen and brought him before the high council.

_____

At this point everyone in the high council stared at Stephen because his face became as bright as an angel's.

Match each term with its description.

3. _____ Martyr

4. _____ Persecution

5. _____ Blasphemy

6. _____ Synagogue of Freed Slaves

A. A person who suffers death as a penalty for witnessing to and refusing to deny his or her faith in Jesus

B. Insulting God

C. Suffering because of one's faith

D. Former slaves who converted to the Jewish faith

Persecution may be harsh or mild. Read each scenario. Answer the questions as a Christian would.

7. Soldiers at Fort Madison often get together to pray before they go on duty. Several other soldiers make fun of them and insult them. How are the Christians persecuted? What would you do in the situation?

_____

_____

_____

8. Students at a local public high school pray in an empty classroom at lunchtime. Some non-Christian students accuse them of holding a religious service on campus and demand that the students stop praying. How are the Christians persecuted? What would you do in the situation?

_____

_____

_____

9. Mr. Abbott was told by his boss that he could no longer pray or read his Bible at work during lunch. The boss said that he would fire Mr. Abbott if he did not stop prayer and Bible reading. How is this Christian persecuted? What would you do in the situation?

_____

_____

_____

10. Christians in some countries may be arrested for worshipping Jesus. How are these Christians persecuted? What would you do in this situation?

_____

_____

_____

_____

Fill in the circle(s) to answer each question.

1. What did Philip and other Christians do because of persecution?
◯ fight back   ◯ give up   ◯ move to other cities   ◯ continue to preach the gospel

2. What happened when Philip preached in Samaria?
◯ He was stoned.   ◯ People believed in Jesus.   ◯ There were healings and miracles.

3. Whom did Philip meet on the road to Gaza?
◯ an angel of the Lord   ◯ a man coming from Jerusalem   ◯ the queen of Ethiopia

4. Why was Philip invited to sit in the carriage?
◯ to explain the Scriptures
◯ to rest from walking
◯ to hide him from persecution

5. How did the traveler respond to the good news Philip shared about Jesus?
◯ He believed and was baptized.
◯ He told Philip to get off the carriage.

6. What happened to Philip after he got out of the carriage?
◯ He ascended into heaven.
◯ He returned to Jerusalem.
◯ The Spirit took him to Azotus.

7. What did Philip continue doing after this event?
◯ preaching the gospel   ◯ persecuting Christians   ◯ riding in strangers' carriages

8. Explain how the prophecy the Ethiopian treasurer was reading in Isaiah applies to Jesus.

_____

_____

_____

9. Write the words to the memory verse. _____

_____

10. Explain how the word *dispersion* relates to your memory verse. _____

_____

_____

11. Acts 8:8 says that there was great joy in Samaria when people heard Philip's message and saw miracles of healing and deliverance. There are many other passages in the Bible that also describe or promise great joy or blessings. What is the cause for joy in the following verses?

	Bible Verse	**Reason to Rejoice**
A.	Luke 2:10–11	
B.	Romans 4:6–8	
C.	Luke 24:51–53	
D.	Psalm 16:11	
E.	Luke 6:22–23	
F.	James 1:2–3	
G.	Jude 1:24	

12. Which of the reasons above do you most appreciate today? Why?

_____

_____

_____

_____

13. Acts 8:39 says that when the Ethiopian man left Philip, he was rejoicing. What made him so happy?

_____

_____

_____

14. God not only gives his people reasons to rejoice, but commands them to do so. Read Psalm 97:12 and Philippians 4:4. What are ways you express your joy in the Lord? Circle your choices.

give thanks   **create art**   **laugh**   *give someone a hug*   throw a party

skip and jump   cLap   **write a poem**   sing and play music   **tell others about him**

serve others in his name   RUN OR SPRINT   raise your hands in the air   share what you have

smile at other people   **give an offering**   *give a high five*   dance

Mark each sentence **T** for true or **F** for false.

_____ **1.** After Stephen was murdered, Saul felt sorry for the Christians. He traveled to Damascus to see if he could find any Christians there to help.

_____ **2.** On the way, Saul heard the voice of Jesus.

_____ **3.** Saul's companions were struck blind.

_____ **4.** Once Saul arrived in Damascus, he did not eat or drink anything for three days.

_____ **5.** A man named *Ananias* heard that Saul was lost and hurried to give him directions.

_____ **6.** Ananias prayed and placed his hands on Saul's eyes so that God would restore Saul's sight and fill him with the Holy Spirit.

_____ **7.** Saul began to preach that Jesus is the Son of God.

_____ **8.** Saul left Damascus and traveled to Jerusalem to meet the apostles.

9. Rewrite the false sentences so that they are true.

_____

_____

_____

_____

Match the statement with the person or people who said it or something similar.

_____ **10.** "Why are you persecuting me?"

_____ **11.** "Isn't this the guy who caused so much trouble?"

_____ **12.** "The Lord Jesus sent me."

_____ **13.** "He really is the Son of God!"

_____ **14.** "He saw the Lord on the way to Damascus."

_____ **15.** "Go over to Straight Street."

_____ **16.** "Who are you, lord?"

| A. Jesus |
| B. Barnabas |
| C. Saul |
| D. Ananias |
| E. The people |

17. What attitude did Saul have when he found out he was wrong?

_____

_____

_____

18. How can you have a similar attitude when you learn you were wrong or

made a mistake? _____

_____

19. Why did the believers in Damascus put Saul into a basket?

_____

_____

_____

20. Courage is the ability to do something difficult, dangerous, or frightening. Explain how each person below showed courage.

a. Ananias: _____

_____

b. Saul: _____

_____

c. Barnabas: _____

_____

Getting Started and Topic 1 | 22.1

1. Write the words of Acts 10:34–35. _____

_____

_____

2. Number the pictures in the order they occurred in the book of Acts.

_____

Peter explained to Cornelius and his family and friends how Jesus had been killed and how God raised him from the dead.

_____

An angel visited Cornelius to tell him to send men to Joppa and to return with Simon Peter.

_____

While Peter was still speaking, the Holy Spirit filled the Gentiles and they began speaking in tongues.

_____

Peter saw a sheet filled with animals. God told him to kill and eat them.

_____

Cornelius welcomed Peter to his home.

_____

Peter protested that he couldn't eat unclean animals. God told Peter not to call unclean what he had called clean.

3. Read Acts 10:9–23. Answer the questions.

a. What was in the sheet in Peter's vision? _____

b. Why did Peter refuse God's command to eat the unclean animals? _____

_____

c. Why did God repeat his command to Peter three times? _____

_____

d. How was the vision of unclean animals related to taking the gospel to the Gentile people?

_____

_____

Use the Word Bank to complete the sentences. Not all words will be used.

Word Bank				
Pentecost	favoritism	Gentile	baptized	centurion
Caesarea	Roman	angel	vision	Holy Spirit
unclean	Simon, a tanner	animals	tongues	convert

4. Cornelius was a _____ officer, living in _____.

5. Cornelius' rank was a _____, with authority over 100 men.

6. An _____ told Cornelius to send servants to Joppa to find Simon Peter because God had noticed that Cornelius was a devout, God-fearing man, who gave generously to the poor.

7. Meanwhile, in Joppa, God sent a message to Peter in a strange _____.

8. Peter had been staying at the home of _____.

9. In Peter's vision, he saw a sheet filled with _____.

10. Peter refused God's command to kill and eat the animals because they were _____.

11. The vision taught Peter that God does not show _____.

12. When Peter spoke to Cornelius and his family, the _____ gave them all the ability to speak in other _____.

13. Speaking in tongues was a gift God gave the church on _____.

14. The new believers were _____ with water.

15. Cornelius was the first Gentile _____ to Christianity.

16. Read the verses about favoritism. Write the verse's reference under the correct column.

Proverbs 24:23   James 3:17   Romans 2:11   1 Timothy 5:21

Be impartial in judgment.	God does not show favoritism.	Keep God's commands without being partial or showing favoritism.	Wisdom is from above; it shows no favoritism.

1. Read Acts 10:34–35 and answer the questions.

a. Who is speaking in these verses? _____

b. What did Peter learn from his vision? _____

c. Whom does God accept—only Jews, or faithful people from all nations? _____

_____

2. Number the sentences in the order they occurred in the book of Acts.

_____ Rhoda heard Peter knocking, but she didn't open the door.

_____ The iron gate that led from the prison into the city opened by itself.

_____ Herod Agrippa ordered the guards to be put to death.

_____ Because Herod wanted to please the Jews, he had Peter arrested.

_____ An angel broke the chains and led Peter out of prison.

_____ Peter was chained between two guards. Other guards were stationed outside.

_____ Once freed, Peter went to Mary's home where Christians were praying.

_____ The Christians opened the door. Peter went to a safe place.

Who did the following actions? Write **Herod**, **Peter**, **an angel**, or **the church**.

3. Prayed for Peter's release _____

4. Told Peter to put on his sandals and coat _____

5. Had Peter arrested _____

6. Knocked at Mary's door _____

7. Read Acts 11:19–21. Underline the words that correctly complete the sentence.

Believers from Cyprus and (Jerusalem, Cyrene) began preaching to the (Jews, Gentiles) about the Lord

Jesus and a large number (believed, doubted) and turned to the Lord.

8. You have studied several characters in the book of Acts. Read the Bible verses first. Complete the chart.

Bible verses: **Acts 11:15–17, Acts 11:22–23, Acts 11:30, Acts 12:23**

Names: **Barnabas, Saul, Herod, Peter**

Character traits: **joyful, prideful, persuasive, trustworthy**

Person's Name				
Character Trait				
Bible Verse				

How can Christians develop godly character? Read the following verses and answer the questions.

9. Romans 5:3–4. How do trials help develop character? _____

_____

_____

_____

10. Philippians 1:11. What does a righteous character produce? _____

_____

_____

11. James 1:2–4. What do trials produce in the lives of believers?_____

_____

_____

1. Write the words and reference for your memory verse. Underline the part that shows how we obtain forgiveness of sins. Double underline the part that shows how people are justified or counted "not guilty" for their sins.

_____

_____

_____

_____

_____

_____

2. Luke tells us that the church in Antioch in Syria included five Jewish and Gentile teachers and prophets. List their names and where they were (or may have been) from.

_____

_____

_____

_____

_____

3. On Paul and Barnabas' first missionary journey, what happened in Paphos?

_____

_____

_____

Fill in the circle(s) to answer each question.

4. From what modern-day country did Paul and Barnabas leave on their missionary journey?
   ◯ Syria   ◯ Turkey   ◯ Jordan   ◯ Greece   ◯ Egypt   ◯ Israel

5. To what modern-day island country did they take the gospel on that journey?
   ◯ Sicily   ◯ Malta   ◯ Corfu   ◯ Cyprus   ◯ Sardinia   ◯ Crete

6. By what means did Paul and Barnabas travel on their journey?
   ◯ by ship on water and by foot on land   ◯ by ship on water and by mules on land

7. List ways God prepared the Roman Empire to be a fruitful mission field for the gospel.

_____

_____

_____

_____

8. What were Saul and Barnabas chosen to do? _____

_____

_____

9. What does the word *proclaim* mean? _____

_____

_____

10. Read each verse. In the column beside it, write what it suggests or commands that God's people should proclaim or make known.

	Bible Verse	**What God's People Should Proclaim**
A.	Deuteronomy 32:3	
B.	Psalm 145:4	
C.	Isaiah 61:1	
D.	Mark 5:20	
E.	Mark 13:10	
F.	Acts 13:38	
G.	2 Timothy 4:2	

1. How did the disciples in Antioch prepare Paul and Barnabas for their first missionary journey? _____

_____

_____

2. Where and to whom did Paul and Barnabas first preach the gospel?

_____

_____

_____

Match the names to the description.

_____ **3.** Bar-Jesus   A. The governor of Cyprus

_____ **4.** Jesus   B. The writer of the books of the law

_____ **5.** John Mark   C. A Jewish sorcerer and false prophet

_____ **6.** David   D. The assistant to Saul and Barnabas

_____ **7.** Sergius Paulus   E. One of the ancestors of Jesus

_____ **8.** Moses   F. The Man whose body did not rot in the grave

_____ **9.** Lucius   G. A church leader in Antioch of Syria

10. What is Bar-Jesus' other name? _____

11. Why did he have two names? _____

_____

12. What two men did Paul and Barnabas meet in Paphos? _____

_____

13. How did they respond to the gospel? _____

_____

_____

14. If you had seen what happened after Paul spoke, would you have believed in Jesus? Why or why not?

_____

_____

_____

15. Read Acts 9:1–8. Who else did the Lord temporarily strike blind?

_____

16. How do you think that Paul might have felt when he saw what the Lord did to the man in the governor's court?

_____

_____

Mark each sentence **T** for true or **F** for false.

_____ **17.** John Mark went with Paul and Barnabas to Pisidian Antioch.

_____ **18.** At the synagogue, the leaders invited Paul and Barnabas to speak to the people.

_____ **19.** Paul spoke about the promises God made to Jewish ancestors.

_____ **20.** Many Jews and converts to Judaism followed Paul and Barnabas.

_____ **21.** Some Jews were jealous and argued against what Paul said.

_____ **22.** Paul and Barnabas decided that they should not preach to the Gentiles.

_____ **23.** The Gentiles were glad to hear the good news and became believers.

_____ **24.** A mob ran Paul and Barnabas out of town, so they went to Iconium.

25. Rewrite the false sentences so that they are true.

_____

_____

_____

26. Read the paraphrase of Acts 13:46. Underline Paul and Barnabas' initial mission. Double underline their second mission.

Then Paul and Barnabas said in a loud voice: "We had to tell you Jews the Good News first. But you did not like the message we gave you from God. Since you do not seem to want eternal life, we will offer it to the Gentiles."

27. Read the paraphrase of Romans 3:29–30. Circle what both Jews and Gentiles must have to be justified before God.

Is God the God only of the Jews? Or is he also the God of the Gentiles? He rules both! Since God is one, he will justify Jews by faith, and Gentiles also by faith.

1. Pretend that you have just picked up a newspaper in Syrian Antioch and it has a news story about Paul and Barnabas' last missionary journey. You notice that some of the facts are incorrect. Draw a line though the facts that are wrong. Below the newspaper, replace the wrong facts with the correct facts from Acts 13. Tell the verse number where you found the correct fact.

DAILY NEWS

No. 49,725   THE BEST SELLING NEWSPAPER IN THE WORLD   Today's Edition

National - World - Business - Lifestyle - Travel - Technology - Sport - Weather

Paul and Barnabas were expelled from Pisidian Antioch, so they traveled along the Via Sebaste to Iconium. When they arrived in Iconium, they went to the Jewish synagogue to speak only to Jews. Through miracles and preaching, some people believed and became Christians. Paul and Barnabas left Iconium and traveled to the towns of Jerusalem and Damascus. There they met a man with crippled feet. The man listened to Paul preach. Paul realized that the man had the faith to be healed, so he said, "Stand up!" The man jumped to his feet and started walking.

The crowd was amazed at the miracle. They decided that Paul was the Greek god Hermes and Barnabas was the Greek god Poseidon. Paul and Barnabas had to tell the people that they weren't gods—they were human beings sent by God to tell the people the good news. Sadly, some Jews arrived and stoned Paul, dragging him out of town and leaving him for dead.

Write the corrected facts and verse numbers below:

a. _____

This fact comes from verse _____

b. _____

This fact comes from verse _____

c. _____

This fact comes from verse _____

Match the Bible verses with the correct pictures.

A. Acts 14:1   B. Acts 14:10   C. Acts 14:13   D. Acts 14 :17   E. Acts 14:19   F. Acts 14:23

2. _____   3. _____   4. _____

5. _____   6. _____   7. _____

Underline the correct word(s) to complete each sentence.

8. Paul and Barnabas were (dedicated/foolhardy/lost) when they traveled from city to city.

9. The Lord gave the missionaries power to (preach and do signs and wonders/govern each city).

10. Paul saw that the man who had never walked had (sinned/faith to be healed).

11. The Lystrans tried to (crown/worship/jail) Paul and Barnabas.

12. The missionaries were (delighted/horrified/unmoved) by the crowd's reaction.

13. After Paul was stoned, Barnabas (went to jail/abandoned him/traveled with him again).

14. On the way home, Paul and Barnabas returned to the (safest/most dangerous) cities.

15. The believers were (angry/encouraged) that Paul and Barnabas returned to see them.

16. Would you have returned? Why or why not? _____

_____

_____

Getting Started and Topic 1 24.1

1. Write the words of the memory verse, 1 Corinthians 1:20. _____

_____

_____

2. Underline the statements that were true of Philippi during Paul's visit.

The city was in Macedonia.   The city had a large Jewish synagogue.

The city welcomed new religions and beliefs.   The city was near a river.

The city was a seaport.   The city was Lydia's home.

The city was on the Aegean Sea.   The city accepted Paul and Silas' message.

3. Complete the definition of a philosopher.

A philosopher is a _____ who _____ various

_____ about _____, right and wrong, and the

_____ and meaning of life.

4. Trace a line through the following cities to show part of Paul's second missionary journey: Antioch in Syria, Tarsus, Derbe, Lystra, Iconium, Antioch in Galatia (Pisidian Antioch), Troas, and Philippi.

Use the Word Bank to solve the riddles. Some of the words will not be used. Some words will be used twice.

Word Bank				
John Mark	Timothy	Paul	Barnabas	Luke
Lydia	Silas	Peter	James	John

5. _____ I am the author of the book of Acts and a faithful companion of Paul.

6. _____ I am the young man who deserted Paul and Barnabas in Pamphylia.

7. _____ I am a young Christian. My mother was Jewish; my father was Greek.

8. _____ I am the missionary who disagreed with Paul.

9. _____ I am the missionary who received a vision calling me to Macedonia.

10. _____ I am a worshipper of God who became a Christian in Philippi.

11. _____ I am the leader of the team with Luke, Timothy, and Silas.

12. _____ I am Paul's partner in ministry whom he chose instead of Barnabas.

13. _____ I am a cloth merchant who gave Paul and his friends a place to stay.

14. _____ I am Barnabas' cousin, who was offered a second chance to serve.

Paul and Barnabas had a disagreement. Read the passages about handling disputes among believers. Answer the questions.

15. Ephesians 4:2–6.

a. How should Christians handle the faults of others?

_____

_____

b. Why should Christians seek unity instead of division?

_____

_____

16. Colossians 3:12–15.

a. With what characteristics should you "clothe" yourself? _____

_____

b. How should you handle a situation where a fellow believer sins against you? _____

_____

c. How should you live with other believers, even those with whom you disagree? _____

_____

Read Acts 16:25–40. Match words spoken with the correct speaker. Answers may be used more than once.

1. _____ "Let those men go. We didn't know they were Roman citizens."

2. _____ "These men are servants of the Most High God, telling you
how to be saved."

3. _____ "These men are teaching customs that are illegal for us
Romans to practice!"

4. _____ "In the name of the Lord Jesus, I command you to come out
of this girl."

5. _____ "Sirs, what must I do to be saved?"

6. _____ "Believe in the Lord Jesus and you will be saved, along with everyone in your household."

7. _____ "Stop! Don't harm yourself. We are all here."

8. _____ "We have been beaten without a trial and put in prison—we are Roman citizens."

| A. A demon-possessed girl |
| B. Paul |
| C. Slave owners |
| D. The Philippian jailer |
| E. Paul and Silas |
| F. The city officials |

9. Sequence the following events in Acts 16.

_____
The jailer believed the prisoners had escaped, but Paul stopped him from taking his life.

_____
A demon-possessed slave girl continued to taunt Paul and his companions.

_____
Paul and Silas sang hymns of praise to God even while in jail.

_____
Paul cast out the demon, but this angered the girl's owners.

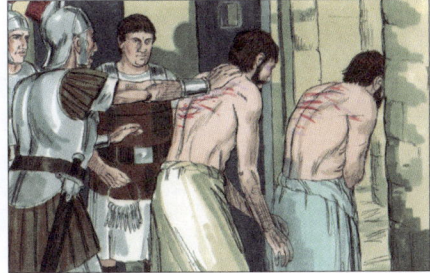

_____
Paul and Silas were beaten and thrown in jail.

_____
The prison doors flew open and the chains of every prisoner fell off.

10. Describe the positive and negative responses to Paul and Silas' preaching and to the gospel in the cities of Philippi, Thessalonica, and Berea. The first one is done for you.

City	Positive Responses	Negative Responses
Philippi	Lydia and the Philippian jailer became Christians as well as their households. They were all baptized.	The slave girl's owners had Paul and Silas beaten and thrown in jail.
Thessalonica		
Berea		

11. Underline the sentences that describe the Jewish people in Berea.

They were open-minded.

They stirred up trouble for Paul and Silas.

They turned the apostles over to the authorities.

They listened eagerly to the apostles' teaching.

They searched the Scriptures.

They wanted to know the truth.

12. Read Jesus' words in John 5:39. Answer the questions.

a. What did Jesus say was the reason people search the Scriptures? _____

b. Whom do the Scriptures point to, or testify about? _____

c. Why do you think so many of the Berean Jews became Christians? _____

_____

1. Answer the questions.

    a. In which city did Paul meet Aquila and Priscilla? _____

    b. What did Paul, Aquila, and Priscilla have in common? _____

    c. Which city did Paul, Aquila, and priscilla go to next? _____

ZEUS / JUPITER
GOD OF THE RAY

HADES / PLUTO
GOD OF DEATH

POSEIDON / NEPTUNE
GOD OF THE SEA

HERMES / MERCURY
MESSENGER OF GODS

APHRODITE / VENUS
GODDESS OF LOVE AND BEAUTY

ARES / MARS
GOD OF WAR

ARTEMIS / DIANA
GODDESS OF THE HUNT

HEPHAESTUS / VULCAN
GOD OF THE BLACKSMITH

ATHENA / MINERVA
GODDESS OF WISDOM

Fill in the circle(s) to answer each question.

2. What troubled Paul about the city of Athens?

    ◯ The people were unfriendly.   ◯ The people rioted.

    ◯ The people worshipped idols.   ◯ There were many philosophers.

3. What happened when Paul debated the Epicurean and Stoic philosophers?

    ◯ They immediately accepted the gospel message.

    ◯ They were healed immediately.

    ◯ They said Paul was preaching about foreign gods.

    ◯ They thought Paul's message was strange.

4. Why did the philosophers take Paul to speak to the high council?

    ◯ He asked to meet with the council.   ◯ They thought Paul was insane.

    ◯ He was teaching about Jewish Law.   ◯ They wanted the council to hear Paul's message.

5. What did Paul say to the members of the high council?

    ◯ He told them about their Unknown God.   ◯ He told them that God created everything.

    ◯ He explained that God would judge the world.   ◯ He spoke about the resurrection.

6. Read Paul's sermon about God and idols in Acts 17:22–39. Make an **X** in the correct column.

	Greek Idols	**One True God**
made of silver, gold, or stone		
live in man-made temples		
created and reigns over heaven and earth		
gives life and breath to everything		
commands repentance		

7. Paul and his friends were tentmakers. Use the clues to complete the puzzle. The last letter of the first word will be the first letter of the next word.

A. Apostle to the Gentiles
B. Town in Acts 14:8 where Paul and Barnabas healed a crippled man
C. Tentmaker and friend of Paul's
D. Book of the Bible in which we learn of Paul's missionary journeys
E. Place of Jewish worship
F. Town where Paul, Aquila, and Priscilla stopped after leaving Cenchrea

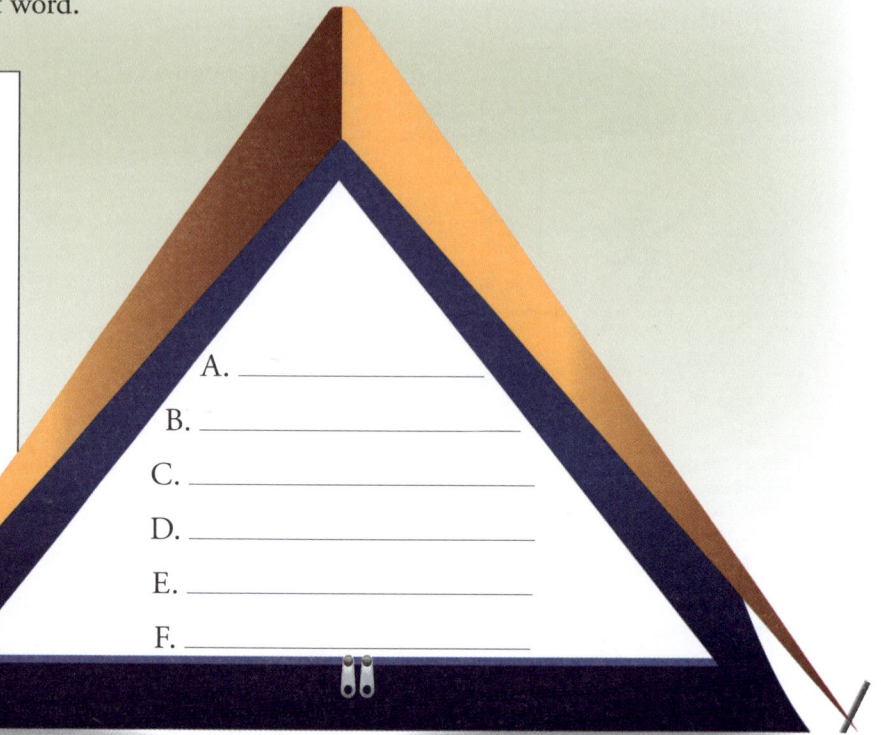

A. _____
B. _____
C. _____
D. _____
E. _____
F. _____

How should Christians work and serve God together? Read the verses and answer the questions.

8. Ephesians 6:7.

   a. What should your attitude be as you work or serve? _____
   _____

   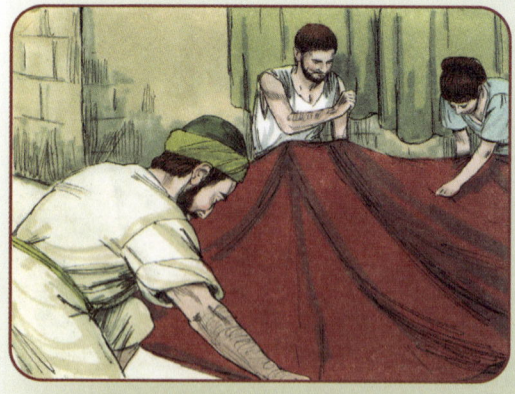

   b. Whom are you really working for or serving?

   _____

9. Ephesians 4:3.

   a. As you work with others, what should you make an effort to keep? _____

   b. What will bind you or bond you together?

   _____

10. 1 Corinthians 15:10.

   a. Who wrote the verse and described himself as a hardworking apostle? _____

   b. Who was working through the author of 1 Corinthians 15:10? _____

   c. If God's grace works through you, should you take the credit for your work? _____

Underline the correct choice to complete each sentence.

1. Paul began his third missionary journey from the church in the city of (Pisidian Antioch / Antioch in Syria).

2. He first visited churches in (Syria, Macedonia, and Judea / Cilicia, Galatia, and Phrygia).

3. He spent three years in (Ephesus in Asia / Macedonia, visiting the cities of Philippi, Thessalonica, and Berea).

4. Next, he visited churches in (Macedonia, Achaia, and Mysia / Phoenicia, Galatia, and Judea).

5. He preached late into the night at (Troas / Miletus).

6. A prophet came to see him in the city of (Tyre / Caesarea).

7. Then, Paul traveled all the way to (Berea / **Jerusalem**).

8. Read your memory verse, Acts 20:24. Answer the questions.

   a. What task did God give to Paul? _____

   _____

   b. What task has God given all Christians? _____

   c. What might we say about the value of our lives in comparison to the task of being a witness for Jesus?

   _____

   _____

Match the person or people to the descriptions.

A. Agabus   B. The man with a demon   C. Paul   D. Christians in Tyre
E. Eutychus   F. The elders from Ephesus   G. Artemis

_____ 9. He heard about a plot to kill him and escaped.

_____ 10. He prophesied to Paul in Caesarea.

_____ 11. He attacked seven Jewish brothers.

_____ 12. They were warned against false teachers.

_____ 13. She was the most popular goddess in Ephesus.

_____ 14. They told Paul what the Holy Spirit had told them.

_____ 15. He was raised back to life.

16. Circle the definition of sorcery.

the power to perform real magic   the use of powerful objects to manipulate evil spirits

the power to command spiritual forces   the use of magical powers obtained from evil spirits

17. Why did many sorcerers believe in Jesus? _____

_____

_____

_____

18. Why did Paul's preaching cause a riot in Ephesus?

_____

_____

_____

_____

_____

19. Why did Paul ask the Ephesian elders to meet him in Miletus? Circle your choice.

He was staying with Philip.   He didn't want to cause another riot.   He was tired of traveling.

20. Why did the Christians in Tyre beg Paul not to return to Jerusalem? _____

_____

_____

21. Who was Agabus and why did he tie his own hands and feet with Paul's belt?

_____

_____

_____

_____

22. Do you think that Paul was right to travel on to Jerusalem despite what he had heard from Agabus and other Christians he met in Tyre and in Caesarea? Why or why not?

_____

_____

_____

_____

1. Read the paragraph. Cross out the sentences that are not part of the Bible story.

Paul taught at the synagogue in Ephesus for three months. Then he moved to the lecture hall of Tyrannus. He did so because it had more room for the crowds who came to listen to him. God performed many miracles through Paul. The seven sons of Sceva, the high priest, decided to imitate Paul. Even though Sceva's sons did not believe in Jesus, they tried to use Jesus' name to free a demon-possessed man. The man beat them up.

Then the man went home naked. The story of what happened spread and many people in the city were afraid. Jews and Gentiles both became Christians. Those who had been sorcerers burned up their magic books in a big bonfire. Because they had wasted so much money, no one wanted to associate with them or listen to the message about the Lord.

2. Rewrite the sentences you crossed out so that they are true.

_____

_____

_____

_____

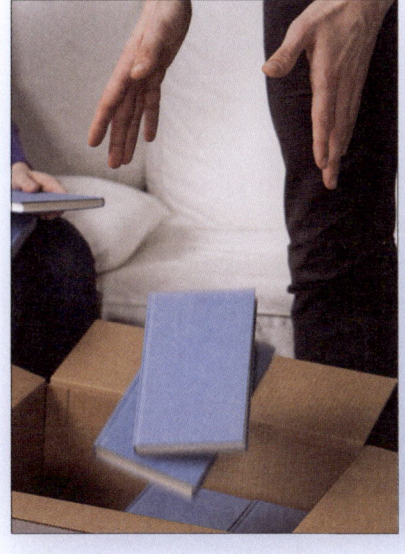

3. Have you ever gotten rid of something because it did not help you grow spiritually? Tell about it. _____

_____

_____

4. Read 2 Corinthians 7:1. Answer the questions.

  a. What should we get rid of? _____

  _____

  b. What should we strive for? _____

  c. Why? _____

5. Circle three things that Demetrius said would happen due to Paul's preaching against idols.

Silversmiths would get a bad reputation.

The temple would lose its influence.

Artemis would destroy the city of Ephesus.

He would have to close his business.

Artemis would be robbed of the honor she deserved.

The temple would become a church.

6. What did the people of Ephesus do when they heard Demetrius? _____
_____

7. Who calmed the rioting Ephesians? What did he say? _____
_____
_____
_____

8. What did Paul do when the riot was over? _____
_____

9. Define sorcery. _____

10. Explain what idolatry is. _____
_____

11. How are sorcery and idolatry alike? _____
_____
_____

Match the sentence to the Bible verse where it is taught.

_____ **12.** Depend on God.   A. Ephesians 6:11–13

_____ **13.** Do not put your trust in idols.   B. Isaiah 45:20–21

_____ **14.** No one but God can save you.   C. Proverbs 3:5–-6

_____ **15.** Use God's power to fight evil spirits.   D. Romans 8:39

_____ **16.** Jesus has power over evil spirits.   E. Leviticus 19:4

_____ **17.** No power is stronger than God's love.   F. Matthew 8:16

1. Explain how the Jews' plot to kill Paul in Greece changed the route of his third mission. _____

_____

_____

_____

_____

2. List the names of the eight men who accompanied Paul back to Macedonia after he fled from Greece. You must read carefully to identify the eighth man.

a. _____   b. _____

c. _____   d. _____

e. _____   f. _____

g. _____   h. _____

3. Seven of Paul's eight companions left him and another companion in Philippi of Macedonia for five days and traveled on to Troas. Who stayed in Philippi with Paul? _____

_____

_____

4. Why did Paul preach to the Christians in Troas all night long? _____

_____

_____

5. Who fell asleep while Paul preached? _____

6. What are some strategies that can help you to stay awake and pay attention if you are sleepy in church, at school, or in another public place? _____

_____

_____

_____

7. What did Paul do after Eutychus fell to his death from the upstairs window? _____

_____

_____

8. When Paul met the Ephesian elders in Miletus, he told them what the Holy Spirit had said would happen to him in the future. Circle what the Spirit said.

that he would be shipwrecked

that he would be arrested and imprisoned

that soldiers would beat him and let him go

that his pursuers would fall off a cliff

9. Read the paraphrase of Acts 20:28–31 below. Underline the commands that Paul gave the elders. Double underline the warnings.

Pay attention to what is going on with you and with all the people the Holy Spirit gave you to lead. Be good shepherds of God's church. He bought it with his own blood! After I leave, ferocious wolves will come in among you. They will prey upon the people. And even from the people you know and trust some will twist the truth to get attention and followers. Watch out!

10. Jesus gave a similar warning to his disciples. Read Matthew 7:15–20. How did Jesus say that his followers would recognize false prophets? _____

_____

11. Read Galatians 5:22–23. What is the fruit of the Spirit? _____

_____

_____

12. Why were the Ephesian elders so grieved when they said goodbye to Paul? _____

_____

1. As Paul traveled to Jerusalem, the Holy Spirit warned him that he would experience hardships and prison. For each passage, Identify the place where the message was spoken, who said it, and what was said to Paul.

   a. Read Acts 21:3–4.

   Place: _____

   Who: _____

   Message: _____

   _____

   b. Read Acts 21:10–12.

   Place _____ Who: _____

   Message: _____

   _____

2. What was Paul's response to the many warnings he received? _____

   _____

   _____

3. Do you think that Paul was right when he chose his course of action?

   Why or why not? _____

   _____

   _____

   _____

4. How should you treat other believers when you disagree regarding God's will? _____

   _____

   _____

5. Read John 17:20–23. Fill in the circle(s) to answer the questions.

   a. What did Jesus want for the church? ◯ unity with one another ◯ unity with God

   b. How did he hope the world would react to seeing this among believers?

   ◯ that they would believe in God ◯ that they would believe Jesus was sent by the Father

Since the church began, until now, many Christians have suffered persecution for their faith. Read Philippians 1:29. Answer the questions.

6. How did Paul suffer nonphysical persecution?

_____

_____

_____

7. How did Paul suffer physical persecution? _____

_____

_____

8. How might Christians suffer persecution today? _____

_____

_____

_____

_____

9. What are some positive strategies in responding to persecution? Circle your choices.

pray for others	take revenge	ask God to smite your enemies	do nothing
try to understand enemies' motives		tell lies and spread rumors about your enemies	
ask God to bless them	get a bodyguard	learn martial arts	get a weapon
ask for justice	defend yourself	trust God cower in fear	ask to dialogue
love your enemies	be patient say nothing	warn others seek to resolve the conflict	
offer money or possessions to be left alone		curse your enemies	ridicule your enemies
put up with the abuse	flee or look for an escape	join those who are persecuting you	

10. Write a prayer for those who are suffering persecution now.

_____

_____

_____

_____

_____

Getting Started and Topic 1

1. Write the memory verse and its reference. _____

_____

_____

_____

Jewish Christians still observed some of the Old Testament traditions. Match the Jewish custom with the verse that describes it.

2. _____ The Passover Feast

3. _____ The Festival of Shelters, or Tabernacles

4. _____ The Nazirite vow

5. _____ Sacrifice after childbirth

6. _____ The Day of Atonement

> A. Leviticus 12:6
>
> B. Leviticus 23:34
>
> C. Exodus 12:47
>
> D. Leviticus 23:27
>
> E. Numbers 6:2–3

7. Read the sentences and write the letter in the correct place on the chart.

A. Paul taught that Gentiles had to convert to Judaism to be saved.

B. Paul taught that Jewish Christians should give up their customs and traditions.

C. Paul taught that salvation was only by faith in Christ Jesus and not by obeying the Law.

D. Paul taught that Gentiles could enter the temple.

E. Paul taught that Roman soldiers were unable to be saved because of their violent jobs.

F. Paul taught that Jews and Gentiles should disobey the Ten Commandments.

True of Paul's Teaching	Untrue of Paul's Teaching

8. Number the pictures in the order they occurred in Acts 21:27–36 and Acts 22:1–29.

_____ Paul told the crowd and explained that he had once persecuted the church by taking letters authorizing the arrest of Christians.

_____ The Roman commander broke up the riot by arresting Paul, but the crowd shouted, "Kill him, kill him!"

_____ In Paul's speech, he retold the story of his conversion on the road to Damascus.

_____ Believing a false rumor that Paul brought a Gentile into the temple, some Jews called for Paul's death. They grabbed Paul and began beating him.

_____ Paul made his defense before the crowd who had tried to kill him, explaining that he was a Jew from Tarsus in Cilicia.

_____ The Roman commander had ordered that Paul be whipped, but the officer stopped him when he learned of Paul's Roman citizenship.

Underline the correct word(s) to complete each sentence.

9. Paul returned to (Jerusalem/Ephesus/Antioch) to report to the church there.

10. Four Christians had completed a (lesson/vow/temple) and were ready to make a sacrifice.

11. When Paul went with the men to the temple, the crowd (grabbed/healed/applauded) him.

12. The commander of the Roman (guard/navy/regiment) arrested Paul.

13. The commander ordered that Paul be taken to (jail/the fortress/the governor).

14. Paul asked permission to (speak to/argue with/agree with) the crowd.

15. Paul told the crowd about his (pastimes/conversion to Christ) and his vision of Jesus.

16. The commander stopped his men beating Paul when he learned Paul was (a Roman citizen/a Jew).

Match Paul's words to the Sanhedrin with the response.

1. _____ Paul said that he had always lived before God with a clear conscience.

2. _____ Paul called the high priest a whitewashed wall or a hypocrite.

3. _____ Paul realized that some council members were Pharisees and some were Sadducees. He told them that he was on trial for his hope in the resurrection of the dead.

4. _____ Paul's words caused a violent conflict.

> A. Ananias, the high priest, told those close to Paul to slap him on the mouth.
> B. Those near Paul warned him that he was insulting the high priest.
> C. The commander took Paul back to the fortress.
> D. There was an uproar.

Paul declared that he was on trial because of his hope in the resurrection. Read the verses about the resurrection below. Answer the questions.

5. John 11:25. Who is the resurrection and the life? _____

6. Acts 4:33. Who testified to the resurrected Christ? _____

7. 1 Corinthians 15:23. Who was the first to be resurrected? _____

When Christ returns, who will be raised? _____

8. 1 Corinthians 15:4–8: About how many people saw Jesus after he was resurrected?

_____

9. Luke 24:4–6. Who went to the tomb, finding it empty?

_____

_____

Who told them that Jesus had risen?

_____

10. 1 Thessalonians 4:13–14. What will happen to believers

who have died? _____

When will we see those believers again?

_____

Use the Word Bank to complete the sentences. Some words will not be used.

Word Bank

oath	Claudius Lysias
nephew	Caesarea Maritima
ambush	prisoner
Sanhedrin	barracks
Felix	militia
charges	priests
Roman citizen	Paul

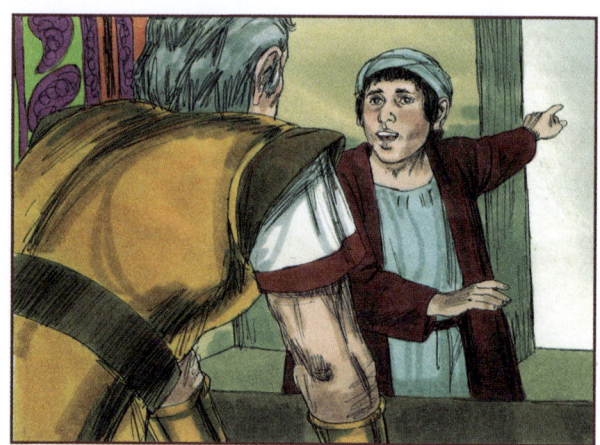

11. The Jewish high council, or _____, was in turmoil.

12. The argument between the Pharisees and Sadducees had become so violent that the Roman commander, _____, returned Paul to prison for his safety.

13. Paul's _____ discovered a plot against Paul.

14. More than 40 Jewish men had sworn an _____ to kill Paul.

15. They planned to _____ Paul the next time he spoke in court.

16. Claudius Lysias wrote a letter to _____, the governor of Judea.

17. The commander told the governor that the _____ against Paul were religious and that Paul's crime was not worthy of imprisonment or death.

18. That night, soldiers took Paul to Antipatris and then on to _____ the next morning.

19. Consider how both the Jews and Romans responded to Paul's message of salvation through faith in the resurrection of Jesus. Make an **X** in the correct column.

	Jews	Romans
took an oath to kill Paul		
arrested Paul in order to protect him		
took Paul to Governor Felix		
did not agree about the resurrection		
respected Paul's Roman citizenship		

Getting Started and Topic 1

1. Write the words of 2 Timothy 4:7–8. Then answer the questions. _____

_____

_____

   a. Who is speaking in this verse? _____

   b. What is the author waiting for? _____

   c. What is the prize or crown that the speaker is talking about? _____

   _____

   d. Do you think the author was aware that he was about to be executed when he wrote this verse? How do

   you know? _____

   _____

2. Number the sentences in the order they occurred in Acts 24.

   _____ Paul admitted that he followed the Way, but he also believed in the God of his ancestors.

   _____ Felix adjourned the hearing, saying that he was waiting for Lysias.

   _____ Felix kept Paul in prison for two years.

   _____ Tertullus, the lawyer for the high council, presented charges against Paul.

   _____ Paul was given a chance to defend himself against the charges.

Write **Lysias**, **Paul**, **Felix**, **Drusilla**, or **Tertullus** to correctly complete each sentence.

3. _____ did not want to hear
   Paul talk about judgment.

4. _____ brought the high
   council's charges against Paul.

5. _____ explained that he
   was on trial because he believed in the resurrection.

6. _____ was the garrison
   commander who first met Paul.

7. _____, Felix's wife, was Jewish.

8. Explain why Governor Felix left Paul in jail and never made a decision about Paul's guilt or innocence.

   _____

   _____

9. Underline the sentences that describe the word *testimony*.

Paul stated his case before Governor Felix.

Felix and his wife, Drusilla, often called Paul to speak with them.

Paul spoke about his hope in the resurrection during his trial before the high council.

Paul wrote letters to the church in Corinth.

Paul was kept in prison for two years.

10. Read 2 Timothy 1:11–12. Answer the questions.

a. Where was Paul when he wrote these words? _____

b. What did God call Paul to do? _____

c. Why do you think Paul was never ashamed of his calling? _____

_____

d. Whom does Paul trust with his future? _____

Match the statement with the reason for each action.

11. _____ The reason the Jews wanted Paul executed

12. _____ The reason the Jews wanted the trial moved to Jerusalem

13. _____ The reason Paul appealed to Caesar in Rome

14. _____ The reason Felix kept Paul in prison

15. _____ The reason Felix often called Paul to speak with him

A. For a bribe
B. To do God's will
C. To ambush Paul
D. As a favor to the Jews
E. To keep Paul from spreading the truth about Christ

16. Pretend you are on trial. A judge wants you to prove that you are a Christian. What testimony could you give as proof?

_____

_____

_____

_____

_____

_____

_____

_____

Use the Word Bank to complete the sentences.

Word Bank					
Caesarea	Roman	Festus	Paul	Bernice	law
King Agrippa	Caesar	innocent	Moses	Christian	God

1. Governor Felix held Paul as a prisoner in the Roman fortress at _____ for two years.

2. When Felix's term of office was over, a new governor, _____, arrived in Caesarea.

3. Almost immediately, the Jews asked the governor to have Paul brought to Jerusalem, claiming he had broken Jewish _____.

4. After eight or ten days, Festus ordered _____ to appear before him.

5. Paul denied breaking any laws, either Jewish or _____.

6. Paul declared that he was _____, and he appealed to _____.

7. Governor Festus did not want to send Paul to Rome without specific charges, so he had Paul appear before _____.

8. King Agrippa arrived with his sister _____.

9. Paul explained that the prophets and _____ taught the truth that the Messiah would suffer and die.

10. King Agrippa interrupted Paul, asking him if he could be persuaded to become a _____.

11. Everything in Paul's life, including his being sent to Rome, was ordained by _____.

RUINS OF THE FORTRESS OF KING HEROD

12. Paul's testimony before Governor Festus and King Agrippa gave evidence of the good news of Christ. Today, many people argue about the teachings of biblical Christianity.

Arguments and facts are listed below. Write the argument and the fact that contradicts it.

- There is no evidence that Christ rose from the dead.
- There is no such thing as sin and no punishment for it.
- There are no such things as miracles.
- Jesus said, "I am the way, the truth, and the life."
- There are many religions so Jesus cannot be the only way to God.
- Over 500 people saw the resurrected Jesus.
- There is no such thing as heaven.
- Peter and John healed a crippled man in Jesus' name; witnesses could not deny the miracle.
- Paul, Peter, and John all affirmed their belief in the existence of heaven.
- Paul stated in his letter to the Romans that sin leads to death.

Argument	Fact

13. Read 2 Timothy 1:8–9. Answer the questions.

a. What should we never be ashamed to do? _____

_____

b. What did God call us to live? _____

c. What did we do to deserve God's grace or favor? _____

14. What is your idea of living a holy life? Write one or two sentences.

_____

_____

_____

_____

1. Read 2 Timothy 4:6–8. Then answer the questions.

   a. To whom does Paul write this verse? _____

   b. What does Paul say is near? _____

   c. What does Paul mean by fighting a good fight and finishing a

   race? _____

   d. Who will claim the prize at the coming of Christ? When will

   they receive the prize? _____

2. Draw the following lines on the map:

   In green, draw a line from Caesarea to Sidon.

   In yellow, draw a line from Sidon to Myra.

   In purple, draw a line from Myra to Cnidus.

   In blue, draw a line from Cnidus to Salmone.

   In red, draw a line from Salmone to Fair Havens.

   In black, draw a line from Fair Havens to Malta.

3. Number the pictures in the order they occurred in Acts 27.

The commanding officer ordered all who could swim to make for land.

The sailors set sail for Phoenix.

The next day, the crew began throwing the cargo overboard.

The sailors bound the hull with ropes to strengthen it.

About midnight on the fourteenth day, sailors threw out four anchors and prayed for daylight.

After throwing out the cargo, they threw the ship's gear overboard.

4. Underline the ways God showed his sovereign will in this lesson.

God told Paul that no one would be lost.

God used Paul to strengthen and encourage the crew.

God spoke personally to the ship's captain.

God saved the lives of all aboard.

God provided a lifeboat for all the sailors.

God sent an angel to encourage Paul.

God saved all the cargo from destruction.

God abandoned all the sailors to their fate.

5. Paul encouraged the passengers and crew. Do you know someone who could use godly encouragement today? Tell how you will encourage that person. _____

_____

_____

_____

Use the Word Bank to complete the sentences. Not all words will be used.

Word Bank					
Publius	Malta	fever	Aristarchus	Rhegium	snake
Appian Way	Puteoli	Jewish	Moses	Forum	God

1. As Paul tried to help warm and dry the shipwreck's survivors, he was bitten by a _____.

2. The people of _____ hailed Paul as a god; _____ invited Paul to stay with him.

3. Paul, Luke, and _____ stayed on the island for three months.

4. When they left the island, their first stop was Syracuse, then _____ and finally to _____.

THE APPIAN WAY

5. On the way to Rome, Paul and his companions met believers at the _____ on the _____.

6. When Paul met the believers, he was encouraged and thanked _____.

Answer the questions.

7. How did Paul show compassion for Publius' father? _____
_____

8. How did Paul show God's loving-kindness to all the people of Malta? _____
_____
_____

9. How can your kind actions help others to know Christ? _____
_____

10. Read Paul's words to the Romans in Romans 2:4. Answer the questions.

a. What is God's kindness meant to lead us to do? _____

b. Do you think God's kindness led the people of Malta to repent and to become Christians? Why or why not? _____
_____
_____

ROMAN FORUM

Fill in the circle(s) to answer each question.

11. How long were Paul and his friends on Malta before they could sail to Rome?

◯ 3 months   ◯ 6 months   ◯ 1 year   ◯ 2 years

12. Where did Paul meet believers in Italy?

◯ The Three Taverns   ◯ Malta   ◯ The Forum   ◯ Puteoli   ◯ Crete

13. To whom did Paul preach in Rome?

◯ to Jews only   ◯ to Gentiles only   ◯ to all who visited him   ◯ to his guard

14. In AD 67, what happened to Paul for a second time?

◯ He was imprisoned in Rome.   ◯ He met with Silas.   ◯ He preached the gospel.

15. Paul ran the good race of faith. Read the paraphrase of 2 Corinthians 11:23–28 from Paul's letter to the believers in Corinth. Underline each way Paul suffered for Christ.

I know I sound crazy, but I've served Jesus by working hard, spending time in prison, being whipped, and facing death. Five different times the Jewish leaders gave me 39 lashes with a whip, and three times I was beaten with clubs. Once I was stoned. Three times I was shipwrecked. I even spent a whole day and a night drifting in the sea. I have traveled a lot and faced dangers crossing rivers and from thieves. I have been threatened with harm by both Jews and Gentiles. And I have faced danger from people who claim to be Christians, but who really aren't. I've endured sleepless nights. I have been hungry and thirsty and have often gone without food. I have shivered in the cold. Yet, my biggest concern is for the welfare of the people in all the churches I and my fellow partners in Christ have started.